It's Time To Tell

GEORGE P. LeBRUN

It's Time To Tell

as told to

EDWARD D. RADIN

William Morrow and Company
New York
1962

To my wife Josephine

Contents

It's Time To Tell

CHAPTER ONE

It Began with Murder

IT BEGAN WITH MURDER.
The address was a rooming house in the raucous Tenderloin. When Coroner Antonio Zucca and I arrived, the body of a woman was sprawled on top of a bed in a sparsely furnished room. A burly man was examining a revolver with what appeared to be clinical interest. I thought he was a detective until a uniformed patrolman explained that the man and the dead woman had rented the room for a daytime tryst. Shortly after they had gone to bed, a second woman rushed in, fired two shots directly into the head of the other, and then fled, dropping the weapon on the floor. As the officer told us this story, the man continued his calm, careful examination of the pistol.

"Who did the shooting?" I asked. The man spoke up for the first time. "My wife," he said. He glanced down at the gun again. "You know, I thought she used the one

I had in my dresser," he remarked, and a note of worry
seemed to creep into his voice as he added, "It looks like
mine, but it isn't."

My career as secretary to the coroner had started; this
was my first case on my first day in office. I had managed
Zucca's recent election campaign and he became the first
Italian to be voted into an important public office in New
York City. I am of French descent, and when Zucca appointed me official secretary, newspaper reporters referred to us as the Foreign Legion of the coroner's office.
Even though my appointment by Zucca had been a personal one and not dictated by the Tammany political
machine, I knew I could be turned out of office at the
next election and looked upon my position as a temporary
one. I was unduly pessimistic. It wasn't until thirty-six
years later, after I had reached the mandatory age limit,
that I reluctantly left the office.

When Zucca, a Democrat, was not re-elected, his successor, Dr. Gustave Scholer, a Republican, asked me to
stay on. Later my post was removed from the political
spoils system and was transferred to civil service.

During my thirty-six years in office I took part in the
investigations of over one hundred thousand accidental,
suicidal and suspicious deaths, including many of New
York's best known murders. Crooked politics, intrigues
and bribes were all part of the setup, and I observed at
first hand the vicious alliance of unscrupulous politicians
with rapacious businessmen who teamed up to interfere
with justice and free the guilty and, on rare occasions,
even convict the innocent.

I saw a few coroners who were for sale to the highest
bidder and watched persons of wealth or importance exert

all kinds of pressure to avoid airing their dirty linens in public. I could have retired wealthy on the bribes offered me. Over the years I fought many varied vested interests as I sought to bring about needed reforms to cut down upon wholly unnecessary deaths. I served under four different boards of coroners, and when that office was abolished in 1918, I became secretary of the succeeding medical examiner's office, carrying on the same work until age, not interest, forced me to retire.

I first entered office with Coroner Zucca on January 1, 1898. New Yorkers had more than the usual reason for celebrating the arrival of this particular New Year. At the stroke of midnight, Greater New York had come into being; the Bronx, Brooklyn, Queens and Staten Island had united with Manhattan to form one city.

My own celebration of the event had to be postponed. As church bells tolled the hour and huge bonfires were set ablaze on the streets, I helped Zucca and the other three newly elected Manhattan coroners take physical possession of the coroner's office. Under the new city charter going into effect at midnight, the new officials were carrying the title of borough coroners. The retiring group had the title of county coroners. We had received a report that these retiring coroners would try a coup and claim they still were in office because no succeeding county coroners had been elected. They did put in an appearance a short time later and demanded that we leave. When the newly elected officials refused, the old coroners directed a police officer on duty in the building to eject us. The farce came to an end when the patrolman suggested instead that they go home and sleep it off. They finally left after vowing to take us to court; they did and lost.

None of the old coroners had run for re-election because the office no longer would be as lucrative. Up to then coroners had operated on a fee basis, receiving payment for each inquest held. Under the new charter, the coroners were being placed on a yearly salary, fixed at six thousand dollars. New Yorkers had discovered the previous year just how remunerative the fee system had been when one of the Brooklyn coroners was arrested for developing a method for increasing the frequency of his fees; the word "racket" was not in use then. He had been called out one day when the body of a floater was found in the East River. He went to the scene, held an inquest at the spot, and paid the police officer a few dollars to move the body to a new location. During the next few weeks there was a sharp increase in the number of bodies found on the Brooklyn side of the river. The rise was so staggering that an investigation was ordered, particularly when it was discovered that none of the bodies had turned up at the morgue for autopsies. The greedy coroner had had the same body dragged from spot to spot along the riverfront and in a short space of time had collected some ten thousand dollars in fees from one bedraggled corpse.

The coroner's office is one of the oldest in existence in the English-speaking world, and it is the oldest continuing office in this country, dating back to very early Colonial days. When William Penn, in 1683, arrived at what is now Philadelphia to govern the young colony, one of his first official acts was to appoint a coroner's court. That same year a coroner's jury investigated the death of a man named Benjamin Acrod and returned with a verdict that he had "killed himself with drink." The penalty for such an offense was the reverting of all his property to the representative of the Crown. Penn was a humane person and he refused his claim in favor of Acrod's heirs.

It was the duty of coroners in New York City to inquire into any sudden, accidental or unnatural death. As secretary to the coroner, it was my job to accompany him to the scene, take notes and participate in the investigation. I also had to summon a coroner's jury and assist the coroner in court when he was holding an inquest. For many years the coroner's court and his private office were located on the first floor of the old Criminal Courts Building. Our corridor was used in bringing prisoners to and from Tombs Prison, which was across the street. An enclosed private bridge led from our building across Franklin Street directly into the Tombs. It was built after mobs attacked guards escorting prisoners through the streets and released the men in custody. The structure became world-famous as the "Bridge of Sighs."

By law, coroners had to hold inquests in all cases except for natural deaths. Lawyers were present by courtesy, but not by right. Few coroners were lawyers, and most of them had little if any conception of legal proceedings. The hearings were informal, witnesses were allowed to ramble; the main purpose was to get information so that a jury could get enough facts to reach an opinion. It became known as the poor man's court. Coroners had the power to make arrests and they could sit as a committing magistrate in cases within their jurisdiction, setting bail for a prisoner. Discharge by a coroner's jury did not always mean the end of a case. A district attorney could order the rearrest of a prisoner and hold him for grand jury action. The prosecutor or one of his assistants would help the coroner question witnesses in homicides.

I learned early the amazing variety of cases that came within the province of the coroner's office. On that same first day we also were called out to investigate the death of a pedestrian—he had been run down by a bicyclist. The standard two-wheel bicycle, as we know it now, was just coming into popularity then, and this was the first case in the city of a pedestrian being killed in such an accident. Although witnesses agreed that the dead man had run into the path of the bicycle and had struck his head on the curb when he fell, it was the custom to arrest any owner of a vehicle involved in an accident and to release him on nominal bail until the inquest. Inquests were held weekly.

The bicyclist was cleared later by a coroner's jury and released. The trysting husband came to see me several days after the shooting, said he was a gambler who recently had come from Chicago to investigate the possibilities of opening a place in the Tenderloin. He was arranging for the surrender of his wife, but since he was a stranger he asked if I could recommend a lawyer. I told him we could not do that in our office. For a stranger, it did not take him long to learn his way. He hired the notorious firm of Howe and Hummel, and when his wife later was placed on trial, a sympathetic jury convicted her of manslaughter and she received a light sentence.

The coroner's court offered far better entertainment than could be seen on any stage. I knew personally some of the great stars of the theater, but few performances by actors could match the spontaneous dramas that rubbed the emotions raw, or the unconscious bits of comedy that went on week after week in our court.

Even deaths from natural causes sometimes brought surprises. For over twenty-five years a man named Murray Hall maintained an employment office on lower Sixth Avenue. He lived with a niece in an apartment behind the agency. He was well known in the neighborhood, was an active member of his local Democratic club, and his favorite recreation was visiting the clubhouse and spending the evening discussing politics and other matters with members. He was about six feet tall and weighed 160 pounds. Hall was considered a "regular fellow" by his friends.

One morning the niece found him dead in bed, the victim of a heart attack. Since there was nothing suspicious about his death, Zucca did not go to the scene, but the coroner's physician did make a routine examination at the house.

The doctor reported that Hall had died of a heart attack and then added, "I think you should know that Hall was a woman."

Because of the unusual circumstances, Zucca decided to hold an inquest. Throughout the hearing the niece always referred to Murray Hall as her uncle. Each time she did, Zucca interrupted to say, "Your aunt," and the girl just as promptly retorted, "My uncle, you mean." She refused to accept the doctor's report that Murray Hall had been a woman, and we were unable to determine if she really did not know of the masquerade.

The coroner's jury found itself troubled with a problem in semantics and solved it with this verdict:

"We find that Murray Hall came to his death by natural causes. He was a lady."

One of the most pathetic incidents occurred when a

ten-year-old girl, the only witness to an ax murder, was
called to the stand. Coroners disliked bringing children
into the court unless it was absolutely necessary, but
there was no choice in this instance. The child was exceptionally bright and pretty with dark brown wavy
hair.

Spectators in the courtroom let out a gasp when the
girl began her story by saying, "I hate to talk against my
papa, but he killed my mama. Papa wasn't always bad,"
she hurriedly offered in his defense. "When he was working and wasn't drinking he used to bring ice in the morning, and used to chop the wood and bring it up for Mama
and me. But sometimes before this last time I have seen
him when he was ugly and drinking and not working and
hit Mama, but not with an ax. Mama was proud and
told me never to say a word about Papa hitting her to
anybody, and Mama stood it a great many times, but
Papa would promise to be good and then would break
his promise.

"You see it was this way. Papa had not been working
for two days and he was ugly and cross and after he
had had his lunch and a pint of beer he went into the
bedroom to sleep. When Mama was busy getting supper
he called her. She told me to tell Papa she was getting
supper for our boarder. He jumped out of bed and put
on his trousers but not shoes, and said he would show
Mama whether or not she would come when he called
her.

"I followed him into the kitchen, and he picked up a
bottle from the table and was going to hit Mama with it,
but I grabbed the bottle and then took all the other bot-
tles and hid them. He hunted around the room and
found the ax which Mama used for cutting kindling wood,

and then he hit her on this side of the face [she indicated the left side of her face to the jury], then on top of the head, and Mama called my name and fell on her face. I ran into the hall screaming and our neighbor came in and put a pillow under Mama's head, and washed off the blood and said, 'She's still breathing.' And then the policeman came, and they sent for an ambulance. Mama never spoke another word to anybody and she died without knowing me again."

The girl then slipped off the witness stand, ran across the room to where her father was seated between two guards, threw her arms around him and sent shivers through all of us when she cried out, "Papa, I don't want you to die; I love you."

I hadn't been with the coroner's office long when I began to appreciate the value of inquests, particularly in accidental deaths. Many buildings then were not equipped with central heating, particularly the lower-priced rooming houses. Whenever there was a cold spell there was a sharp rise in deaths from gas asphyxia. Many of these roomers, whether they had kitchen privileges or not, would buy small hot-plate stoves, attach them to the gas jets in their rooms, and keep them burning all night during cold weather. Escaping gas would kill them, and now and then explosions would wreck buildings when somebody would smell the fumes and light a match.

At first we thought these deaths were due to faulty connections of the hose to the jet and the burner, and newspapers printed our warning to make certain that the hoses fitted tightly. But the death toll continued to climb that winter with more than eight hundred, many of them in Brooklyn.

Coroner Scholer and I went out on some of these calls and we noticed that the hoses attached to the stoves seemed to be thin, not as heavy as the rubber tubing that was attached to gas heaters in our homes. Tests were made on these hoses and it was found that they were not airtight, that gas vapors could seep through the porous construction. The facts were presented at an inquest, and the jury recommended the enactment of a local ordinance establishing minimum standards of safety for gas hose. The board of aldermen quickly passed such a law, and police were sent out to stores to confiscate all unsafe hose. People who had bought the cheap hose were alerted to the danger, and deaths from this type of accidental gas poisoning showed a prompt decline.

During the construction of the first subway tunnels under the East River to Brooklyn, many of the sandhogs were being killed on the job. Since it is dangerous work, their deaths were being attributed to the "bends," an occupational hazard caused by passing too quickly into normal air from the compressed air used in the caissons. Autopsy surgeons, though, found that the bends was not the sole cause of death for some of the victims, that there were additional contributing causes such as tuberculosis or other organic diseases. These victims were physically ill men who were really killing themselves by undertaking the work they were doing; they simply did not have the physical stamina for withstanding the high air pressures necessary in the caissons.

An inquest disclosed that the construction company was so anxious for manpower that it was hiring anyone who applied for a job. No physical examinations were made of the men, and they were sent right down to the caissons as soon as they were hired. The pay was high for that period, ten dollars a day, and men anxious to provide well for their families were snapping at the lure. The jury followed the advice of the coroner and in its verdict suggested that any man hired for sand-hog work pass a thorough medical examination. A copy was sent to the contracting firm and, to its credit, it promptly placed a physician on the job site to examine all applicants. There was a satisfactory decrease in the number of sand hogs being killed on that construction job, and, as a further result, a law was passed making such examinations mandatory.

While these are examples of how properly conducted inquests can be put to good purposes, I also saw, at the close of my first year with the coroner's office, the other side of the coin, where an inquest was misused to build up public opinion against a suspect in one of the most celebrated murder cases of the Gay Nineties. It was a flagrant abuse of the coroner's court, and an innocent man was almost electrocuted. Many people today, unaware of the actual facts, still believe this man was guilty. I have read many accounts of this case in various books and publications, but none has contained any of the information about what took place in our office and later in the coroner's court.

But to counterbalance it, this soon was followed by another case in which our office may very well have prevented a grave miscarriage of justice. I am now going to give you the full facts, including information never before published, on both of these cases.

CHAPTER TWO

Two Faces of Justice

I HAD LOOKED FORward to spending a quiet day in the office on December 28, 1898. Coroner Zucca was off duty and it was a good opportunity for me to catch up on paper work. It was a gray, overcast morning, gaslights were lit, and the streets were still filled with snow from a pre-Christmas storm, making walking treacherous. I had just settled down in my office when Coroner Edward Hart poked his head in the door and asked that I work with him.

Because the other official secretaries to the coroner were political appointees who often had chores to perform for their district leaders, I frequently was called upon to serve all four coroners. Reporters were so accustomed to see me working with the different officials that they referred to me in print as secretary to the "board of coroners." Technically there was no such office, but in reality I was serving that function.

It was late morning when we received a report that Mrs. Katherine Adams of 61 West Eighty-sixth Street had been poisoned. While Coroner Hart and I were struggling into our overshoes, Assistant District Attorney John J. McIntyre hurried into the office with Harry S. Cornish, physical director of the Knickerbocker Athletic Club, who, he said, had unwittingly given the poison to Mrs. Adams. Since it was a police matter, we were joined by George McClusky, head of the detective division.

Cornish was a tall, well-built man, with the appearance of an athlete who kept himself in trim. He boarded at the Adams home, having moved there earlier that year, and said he was a friend of Mrs. Adams and her daughter, Mrs. Laura Rogers, who was separated from her husband and living with her mother. The rest of the household included an elderly woman, distantly related, and the servants. This is the verbatim statement Cornish made in the coroner's office to us. He was allowed to tell his story without interruptions, and spoke slowly, selecting his words with care:

"This morning Mrs. Adams awakened and complained of a severe headache. She hunted around the house for a remedy and could find nothing. I then recalled that on Christmas Eve I had received through the mail a small bottle of Bromo Seltzer, contained in a rather expensive and elaborately worked filigree silver case, a typical Christmas present.

"I hadn't the faintest idea who had sent it since there was no accompanying card. As a matter of fact, I suspected it might be an expensive joke on me from one of the men at the club—sending me a hang-over remedy, you see. I had shown it to Mrs. Adams when I first brought it

home, and she had admired the artistic quality of the filigree work. She agreed when I suggested that she try a glass
of it for her headache. So I poured out a teaspoonful
into a glass of water, stirred it up, and handed it to her
while it was still effervescing.

"She drank the greater part of it and then placed the
glass on the table, remarking suddenly that it had a
strange taste. I picked up the glass and tasted what remained, noticing that it had a strong odor. Hardly had
I put the glass back on the table and before I could say
anything, Mrs. Adams screamed, fell to the floor and
rolled around in agony, beating her hands against the
rug."

Cornish paused at this point to rub his hand across his
forehead. He then continued.

"Mrs. Rogers and I ran to her, lifted her from the floor
to a couch. Then we sent a maid running for the nearest
doctor. By the time he came, and that was very soon, she
was in a coma. He examined her for an instant, saw that
her condition was hopeless and asked for the Bromo
Seltzer glass. Dipping his finger into the remaining liquid,
he tasted it. It was only a short time ago since I had taken
a sip of the liquid and I was feeling ill myself. After this
sampling the physician declared the liquid contained cyanide and that, unquestionably, Mrs. Adams had been
poisoned. And almost as he finished speaking she died.
That is exactly what happened this morning."

Chief McClusky pointed out to Cornish that the poison
seemed to have been intended for him. Coroner Hart
asked him if he could think of anyone who would want
to kill him.

Cornish shook his head. "I didn't think I had any

enemies. Certainly none who would want to murder me. It is sort of hard to imagine such a thing. It is all so sudden."

Pressed further as to whether he had trouble with anybody, he stated he had difficulties with Roland Molineux at the Knickerbocker Club. He again spoke slowly and carefully as he discussed the incident:

"Well, we quarreled there one day over some accusations I had made against him to the board of governors. He came back with some countercharges against me. I was pretty mad because, after all, he was one of the club governors and a member of the board. There was an investigation of my charges and his countercharges and then, as I might have expected, the board decided that I should make a written apology to Molineaux for what I had said. That should have ended the matter but, apparently, he was still angry, for even after I sent him the apology he resigned and joined the New York Athletic Club."

With the mention of Molineux's name it became evident why McIntyre had suggested that the head of the detective bureau be brought into the case. The Molineux family was wealthy and socially prominent. Roland's father was General Edward L. Molineux, head of C.T. Reynolds, one of the largest manufacturers of dyes in the country, and Roland Molineux was successful in his own right. He had studied chemistry and while still a young man became superintendent of a large chemical firm in Newark, New Jersey, that made dry colors. He also performed in shows as a star gymnast, a popular amateur sport at that time.

Just the previous month, on November 29, Molineux

had married Blanche Cheseborough, a vivacious brunette, who was soloist at a fashionable church.

Questioned further, Cornish said the package had been mailed to him at the Knickerbocker Club. There had been a gift envelope inside, but no card was enclosed. He said he did not recognize the handwriting of the sender but had saved the wrapping paper. The silver holder and the blue bottle were in a Tiffany box. Although Cornish did not accuse Molineux, he offered no other name.

Coroner Hart and I went to the house where we interviewed Mrs. Rogers. Her story of her mother's death was similar to the statement given to us by Cornish. She said that when he went to his room to get the gift bottle, he first gave it to her, but when she had difficulty breaking the paraffin seal, he took over, opened the bottle, and poured the powder into a spoon. I took possession of the bottle, and when I removed the cap there was a noticeably strong odor. The coroner's physician later reported that the bottle was loaded with cyanide crystals.

The inquest was delayed while police began an investigation. The delay was somewhat unusual because one of the purposes in holding an early inquest was to get statements from witnesses under oath while all the facts still were fresh in their minds. Police, of course, had the power to make an arrest at any time regardless of an inquest, and a district attorney was not bound by the verdict of a coroner's jury. Any time he felt he had a case against a suspect he could present his information directly to a grand jury and seek an indictment. On the surface the delay seemed meaningless and unimportant.

Detectives learned that Tiffany had not sold the silver filigree holder. They were able through a hallmark on the piece to trace it to the manufacturer, and his records showed that it had been shipped to a jewelry store in Newark not far from the factory where Molineux was employed. A clerk recalled selling the holder on December 21 to a tall man who had a red beard and spoke in a deep gruff voice. The description of the buyer did not match Molineux, and when the clerk later saw the chemist he said he was not the man who had purchased the silver holder.

Reporters soon had the story, and the Molineux name made it important news. They learned that Molineux and Cornish had first quarreled in April, 1897, over an amateur circus the club was staging. Some months later Cornish had written a letter to an athlete in which he had made disparaging remarks about the director of another organization on interclub matters. Molineux was shown the letter and he asked the board of governors to dismiss Cornish for this breach of manners. The board apologized to the other man involved but kept Cornish on. Shortly after that, club members heard Cornish taunt Molineux and call him a vile name, but the chemist laughed and walked away. The final break came when Cornish wrote letters to members of other clubs in which he derided Molineux's athletic ability and character. He told the house committee chairman that Molineux was selling rum and was associated with a house of prostitution. This seemed to be the final straw for Molineux, who informed the secretary of the club that Cornish had to be discharged or he would resign. When nothing was done, Molineaux did resign in December, 1897, a full year before Cornish received the blue bottle in the mail. Members of the club said that while Cornish was impulsive, liked to have his own way and was often tactless, he was a good coach and they did not want to lose him.

I would like to point out that the story Cornish told at the coroner's office was at variance with this information.

Further sensations for newspaper readers soon were provided when police revealed they also were investigating the recent death of Henry C. Barnet, a broker, and a close friend of Molineux. They suspected that he had also died of poisoning. Both men were linked to Blanche Cheseborough. Molineux had met her in the summer of 1897 on a cruise in Maine. He had proposed to her on Thanksgiving Day that year, but she had not accepted. Later that fall he had introduced her to Barnet and after that both men had begun taking her out.

She finally ceased seeing Barnet and then in early October, 1898, accepted Molineux's renewed proposal. Barnet, who had continued living at the Knickerbocker Club after his friend had moved out, became ill on October 30, and the club doctor had thought he exhibited the symptoms of diphtheria. Barnet had said he felt ill after taking a dose of Kutnow powders that had come in the mail. The doctor had had the powders analyzed and they had been found to contain cyanide of mercury. Barnet had refused to discuss it. He appeared to be recovering when he died suddenly on November 10, nineteen days before the marriage of Blanche Cheseborough and Molineux. In signing the death certificate, the doctor attributed it to heart failure caused by diphtheria.

Police also learned that some months earlier a man had rented a letter box in a store under the name of H. C. Barnet and among the mail had received various samples of patent medicines. The storekeeper identified Molineux as the box holder. Captain McClusky told reporters, "The same mind sent both poisons."

No arrest had been made by the time the delayed inquest opened on February 9, 1899. It was no secret that Molineux was the chief suspect. He was under subpoena and he came accompanied by a lawyer. Assistant District Attorney McIntyre appeared for his office, and Coroner Hart presided. The coroner was typical of many of those who held the office. He was an amiable man, personally honest and a steadfast machine politician. He knew little about the functions of the coroner's court or of law.

Molineux was called to the stand, and the questions asked by McIntyre established thoroughly that he and Cornish had quarreled and that he had sought to have the other discharged. The prosecutor also brought out information to the jury that Molineux was a chemist, that he had his own private laboratory at the factory, that it was possible for him to manufacture poisons from the raw materials available in the factory, and that the plant was located near the jewelry store where the silver filigree holder was bought. With these and similarly selected questions, McIntyre ended his examination. When Molineux's lawyer arose to question his client, McIntyre objected and told Coroner Hart that it was his right to prevent any cross-examination. The coroner did have this power. He also had the right, though McIntyre did not mention it, of preventing the district attorney from asking any questions. Given the "law" by McIntyre, Hart sustained the objection.

The ruling completely negated the very reason for holding an inquest, which was to obtain all the information.

By limiting the questioning to just one side, which could and did ask questions designed not to bring out all the facts but to give an impression, the inquest was turned into a farce under the cloak of legality.

From that point on, McIntyre completely dominated the proceedings. Neither the coroner's jury nor the reporters present knew that he and Cornish were close personal friends, that after Mrs. Adams died Cornish had not notified police but had gone all the way downtown to see his friend, and that we were not notified of the death until McIntyre and Cornish were getting ready to enter our office.

When Cornish took the stand, he told of receiving the package in the mail, and once again his quarrels with Molineux were emphasized. He added gratuitously that he bore Molineux no ill will, which hardly explained his active letter writing. Seven experts hired by the district attorney's office took the stand and all testified that it was Molineux's handwriting on the wrapper Cornish had saved.

Although the inquest had been called specifically to inquire into the death of Mrs. Adams, McIntyre not only broadened it to include Barnet, but, in fact, spent more time on Barnet's death than on the other. Leaving no doubt that Barnet had been murdered, he soon supplied black headlines for the press by inferring that it was the rivalry over the favor of Blanche Cheseborough that had led Molineux to murder his friend. He dragged her through the mire by inferring that she had been Barnet's mistress and that Molineux got his revenge.

When she took the stand and denied that she had ever

had intimate relations with Barnet, a letter she had written to him, found in his desk, was read to the jury:

"I am distressed to learn of your illness. I arrived home Saturday and am so exceedingly sorry to know that you have been indisposed. Won't you let me know when you are able to be about? I want so much to see you. Is it that you do not believe me? If you would but let me prove to you my sincerity. Do not be cross any more. And accept, I pray you, my very best wishes. Yours, Blanche."

While the letter may sound somewhat innocuous to the casual reader, it was read with voice inflections that gave an impression that it was an ardent demand for an instant assignation.

The inquest stretched out from February ninth to the twenty-seventh, with each day supplying fresh sensations, and the factual accounts of the one-sided material presented in court built up an impression of Molineux as a Borgia-like creature who went about poisoning people he disliked. Molineux's lawyer was firmly gagged during the entire time, not allowed to ask any witness a single question. The climax came when McIntyre even took over the coroner's role and charged the jury. It was a typical prosecutor's demand for a guilty verdict, but instead of asking that they find Molineux guilty, he asked them to consider from the evidence whether Molineux should be held for the grand jury. It was not surprising that the coroner's jury returned with a verdict that "The death of Katherine Adams was caused by cyanide poisoning, administered to her by Harry Cornish, said poison having been sent through the United States mail to Harry Cornish by Roland Molineux."

With the recommendation by the coroner's jury,

Molineux was quickly indicted and sent to the Tombs to await trial. It was only *after* the inquest that somebody in the district attorney's office may have realized that the only fact on record about Barnet's death was a certificate signed by a reputable physician that he had died of natural causes. The following day his body was exhumed, and this was followed by more headlines when the prosecutor's office announced that a toxicologist had found cyanide in his body.

Mrs. Adams had died on December 28. The investigation went on for over a month with all information released to reporters pointing toward Molineux. The coroner's court inquest lasted almost as long with only information pointing to Molineux being presented. There is little doubt that Molineux was thoroughly tried in the press, and public opinion had convicted him before he even was indicted and placed on trial. The result of his trial was a foregone conclusion. He was found guilty and sentenced to die in the electric chair.

Two episodes in his trial deserve mention. The number of handwriting experts had risen from seven at the inquest to fourteen at the trial. The quantity may have been an indication of what the prosecutor thought about the quality. The scientific study of handwriting was in its infancy then, and while there were many self-styled experts, there were few really qualified men. Most of the state's experts did not even attempt to offer any scientific reasons for their opinion that Molineux had addressed the package to Cornish. They simply said it looked like his handwriting. The defense, on the other hand, had employed D. N. Carvalho, one of the few court-recognized experts in the field. He demonstrated that the curves and angles of the writing on the package were completely dissimilar to Molineux's handwriting and testified flatly that Molineux had not written the address. The jury may have been impressed by the quantity.

District Attorney Asa Bird Gardiner headed the prosecution. His sole claim to fame was the classic remark he made the night Tammany Hall was voted back into power and swept him into office: "To hell with reform." The character of the prosecution perhaps can be best summed up by one of the closing remarks by the prosecutor. Molineux had been indicted only for the murder of Mrs. Adams, although the court, over the objections of the defense, allowed testimony to be brought in about Barnet. The motive for the attempted murder of Cornish that backfired into the death of Mrs. Adams, if Molineux did it, obviously was the long enmity between the two men. Witness after witness told of their quarrels. All of these revolved about Knickerbocker Club affairs only. They began before Molineux had met Blanche Cheseborough, and she certainly was no part of their quarrels. Yet in his summation the prosecutor pointed to Blanche Cheseborough Molineux who sat beside her husband and shouted dramatically, "There sits the motive!"

Molineux was in the death house for twenty months while his case was on appeal. In a unanimous decision, the court of appeals reversed the conviction and sharply criticized the many legal errors, including the admission of any testimony about the death of Barnet. The court also had equally caustic things to say about the quality of the testimony of the state's handwriting experts.

It was almost four years since the death of Mrs. Adams when Molineux's second trial finally ended. The case

this time was presented by a new district attorney who
had come into office, William Travers Jerome, still recognized as one of the most honest and forthright prosecutors
in the city's history. The case was presented fairly; the
defense was virtually the same, a complete denial. Molineux was acquitted.

The long years he had spent in jail had taken their toll.
He was a broken and bitter man. His wife obtained a divorce the following year and later married the lawyer
who had represented her. Molineux turned to writing
articles and plays about the unfortunate lot of convicts,
and Belasco produced one of his plays, *The Man Inside*.
It closed after only a few performances. Molineux married his secretary on November 7, 1913, and had a child,
but within two years his mind was broken and he was
committed to an institution. He died there on November
2, 1917.

The acquittal of Molineux still leaves open two questions.

What about the death of Barnet? Frankly, I believe he
died of natural causes. Cyanide is one of the swiftest-acting
poisons known. The collapse of Mrs. Adams within moments of drinking the poison is a typical cyanide death.
And even a very small dosage is usually fatal. If Barnet
had died of cyanide, as the district attorney's office announced, then he would have had to receive the fatal
dose the day he died. That would completely eliminate
Molineux as a suspect. One of the points the prosecution
used against him in trying to show that he no longer was
friendly with Barnet was that he did not visit him during
his illness. Molineux explained that he stayed away because he was told it was diphtheria. The disease is highly

contagious and at that time frequently resulted in death. It is interesting to note that the prosecution, with one exception, failed to produce any witness who could mention the slightest disagreement between the two friends. The one exception was Cornish, who claimed Barnet once returned from a planned yachting trip because he had found Molineux on board. The prosecution went far afield in claiming that Molineux was jealous of Barnet because of Blanche Cheseborough. The last time she had gone out with Barnet was in June, 1898. She agreed to marry Molineux in October. Barnet did not become ill until the end of October. A man rarely poisons his rival after he has won the girl and is on the eve of his wedding to her.

Who tried to poison Cornish? Police, and most certainly the district attorney's office, considered but one possibility. Neither Cornish nor Mrs. Rogers was investigated. I am not making any accusations, but since elaborate schemes in which a person sends a death threat to himself are not unknown, police should have checked it through. Cornish and Mrs. Rogers were friendly. If Mrs. Adams had objected to their friendship, then she might have been the intended victim after all. Cornish was a divorced man; Mrs. Rogers was separated from her husband. Such situations have been the cause for murder. Another motive for the attempted murder of Cornish might have been found in his relationship with other members of the club. Molineux was not the only one who disliked him. Police did learn that a second letter box had been rented in another store by a man using Cornish's name, and this man also had been receiving samples of medicines. This news was released with a fanfare of publicity to throw further suspicion on Molineux, but what was kept quiet was that the shopkeeper was brought to look at Molineux and stated definitely that he was not the man who had rented the box under the Cornish name. Molineux was not the man who had purchased the silver filigree holder. Club members knew where Molineux worked and certainly knew of the ill will between him and Cornish. A club member could have sent the poison to Cornish hoping to shift the blame on Molineux. Finally, the poison was mailed to Cornish during the first month of Molineux's marriage. It is a rare bridegroom who is busy concocting elaborate murder plots during the first weeks of his honeymoon.

We have never come nearer to a solution than when we first heard the strange story in the coroner's office. But I am certain of one thing: had it not been for the one-sided inquest, Molineux never would have been indicted for the murder. The failure of police to make an arrest was a good indication that they did not believe they had sufficient evidence to warrant it. The inquest had been delayed so it could be used as a forum to get a coroner's jury to make the recommendation, and the hearing did build up public opinion against Molineux. It was one of the most biased and unfair public inquiries I witnessed in my thirty-six years with the office.

Even while Molineux was appealing his conviction, the coroner's office became involved, indirectly at first, in another and equally sensational case of suspected poisoning. I also had a casual connection with the case that later became important. But where Molineux's conviction represented to me an abuse of a coroner's inquest, the work of the coroner's office in this second case, after conviction, was the reverse.

The news report of the death of William Marsh Rice, an eccentric millionaire, was just another item on the obituary page as far as our office was concerned. Rice, who was eighty-four years old, had come to New York after amassing a huge fortune in Texas. He was a recluse and lived with his valet-nurse, Charles Jones, in a large house at 500 Madison Avenue. He was on bad terms with some of his relatives, had a fear of being poisoned, and did his own cooking. His dietary habits were most unusual, particularly for a man his age; shortly before his death he had eaten nine bananas, five fried and four raw. His doctor certified that death was due to "old age, a weak heart and diarrhea."

Several days later the district attorney suddenly issued an order forbidding the funeral and asked our office to conduct an autopsy on the already embalmed body. Meanwhile, the prosecutor had ordered the arrest of Albert T. Patrick, Rice's lawyer, on a forgery charge.

Dr. Donlin, a surgeon on our staff, performed the autopsy. Dr. Hamilton Williams, another coroner's physician, happened to be in the morgue at the time and watched the autopsy.

I recall very well that day. Dr. Williams had just returned to our office from the morgue where he had been with Dr. Donlin and mentioned watching the autopsy. Since I was curious, I asked him his opinion.

"There's nothing to it," he told me. "The old boy died of old age. He ought to have died years ago."

His remarks were in disagreement with the findings of Dr. Donlin, who reported to the district attorney that he had found some general congestion in the millionaire's lungs that might have been the result of some irritant poison. Dr. Williams thought the congestion was in keeping with the aged man's general condition.

Dr. Williams was an unusual character. Well over six feet tall and weighing more than two hundred pounds, he wore a neatly trimmed Van Dyke, a mustache, and was never seen without his tall silk hat. Born and educated in Ireland, he spoke fluent French and Italian. He had served for a time with the British Army and later practiced medicine in Dublin. A few hours after the Phoenix Park assassination of Lord Cavendish, he treated one of the fleeing killers for a broken leg and, fearing arrest for this act, he also fled the country, escaping to France. He finally made his way to the United States, where he became a close friend of a Tammany Hall district leader; his appointment as a coroner's physician was a political one.

With the report from Dr. Donlin, the prosecutor charged Patrick with the murder of his wealthy client and revealed his reasons for stopping the funeral.

Rice had died on Sunday night, September 23, 1900, but no public announcement was made. The following morning Patrick went to one of Rice's banks and presented a check for $25,000 made out to him and signed by Rice. There was nothing unusual in this procedure. Rice frequently drew checks to Patrick, even in the six figures, since the lawyer fronted for the millionaire in various stock deals. The teller noticed that the check had been made payable to "Abert T. Patrick," without the letter, *l*. Patrick had endorsed it with his correct name on the back. It was a minor error, but the bank teller wanted verification. He telephoned Rice's home and was told by

Jones, the valet, that he had written out the body of the check and Rice had signed it. When the teller insisted upon talking to Mr. Rice, Jones told him the millionaire was dead.

The teller refused to cash the check, retained it and notified his superiors, who decided to place the facts in the hands of the district attorney. The prosecutor called in a handwriting expert, who said Rice's signature had been traced and that it was a forgery. Patrick then was arrested, the funeral was stopped and the autopsy ordered.

The valet, Jones, also was arrested for the murder. He told several conflicting stories. At first he confessed that he had killed Rice by saturating a towel with chloroform and holding it over the aged man's face until Rice died. He said Patrick had not been present but that the lawyer had induced him to do so and he was under Patrick's influence. He then changed his story and said he had seen Patrick holding a towel over Rice's face as he lay on his bed and that the lawyer had murdered his master. He then switched back to his original story. Jones had been hired by Rice for his strength rather than for his mental ability.

The prosecutor accepted the first and last confession as the true ones, that Jones killed Rice under Patrick's orders. The prosecutor was certain that he had found an excellent motive for the murder. Rice's latest will left generous bequests to relatives, a grant of $250,000 to a small Texas college, with the bulk of the fortune left to Patrick—over ten million dollars! It was a very strong motive for murder, particularly since in a previous will Rice had left most of his fortune to the college. And when a fortune of ten million dollars is at stake, many strange

things can happen, and many strange things did happen
in this case.

There was one serious flaw in the prosecutor's case—
had Rice actually been poisoned or had he died of old
age? Dr. Donlin's autopsy report said that the congestion
in Rice's lungs could have been caused by an irritant
poison like chloroform, not that it had been.

The case then took a very surprising turn, at least for
me. Dr. Williams asked for a leave of absence from the
coroner's office so that he might devote his entire time to
the Rice case. He explained that he had been retained
by the prosecution as an expert witness who had been
present at the autopsy and examined the congested lungs.

The sudden emergence of Dr. Williams as an expert
witness for the prosecution was startling for several reasons. First, on the day of the autopsy he had told me very
flatly that Rice had died of natural causes. It was difficult
to imagine that the district attorney had retained him to
swear on the witness stand what he had told me in the
office.

Also, while Dr. Williams was a capable medical doctor
and a great storyteller, he was in no way a post-mortem
specialist. As I indicated earlier, his appointment had been
made at the personal request of a Tammany Hall district
leader and not upon his qualifications. He was not a
pathologist, had little autopsy experience before his appointment, and had performed only a few autopsies in the
three years he had been in office. Even on these he found
himself in sharp conflict with the more experienced members of the medical staff, who often disapproved of his
methods of performing autopsies. Many of his findings
were successfully challenged.

Just the same, when the case came to trial, Dr. Williams was one of the mainstays of the prosecution. He took the stand and testified under oath that Rice's death had been caused by chloroform poisoning. I never knew why he changed his views as to the cause of Rice's death. It is a fact that he was paid an $18,000 fee as an expert witness by the district attorney's office. This represented some three times the salary he received for an entire year's work as a coroner's physician.

With this testimony, the autopsy report, the story told by Jones and the ten-million-dollar will, the prosecution had little difficulty in speedily convicting Patrick of first-degree murder.

While the case was under appeal, there occurred a dramatic incident that a fiction writer would have hesitated to invent. The more experienced autopsy surgeons in the coroner's office had been uneasy about the testimony of Drs. Williams and Donlin at Patrick's trial. They felt the autopsy findings were too sketchy to say with any certainty that Rice's death had been due to chloroform poisoning. In fact, they felt there was not even scientific proof that chloroform had been administered; only the changeable stories by Jones. Proof that it was a murder had rested solely upon the testimony of the doctors.

One day a man named Giovanni Ferrari was found murdered. He had been tied securely and killed with chloroform. The bottle, the rags, everything used, had been left at the scene by the fleeing killers.

Dr. Philip O'Hanlon, one of the most skilled autopsy surgeons in the office, was assigned to the case. Realizing that this murder presented a perfect opportunity for a clinical study of chloroform poisoning, Dr. O'Hanlon invited Dr. John H. Larkin, adjunct professor of pathology at the College of Physicians and Surgeons of Columbia University, to work with him. Many other prominent pathologists attended to watch and study for themselves.

These highly skilled men found that the condition of Ferrari's lungs differed from the description in the autopsy on Rice. Large sections of Ferrari's lungs were not congested at all, conditions in the anterior and lateral regions being quite normal. Other tests proved the presence of chloroform.

As a result of these findings more than five hundred physicians signed a memorandum forwarded to the court of appeals urging a new trial for Patrick on the ground that the testimony of Drs. Williams and Donlin had been at odds with medical knowledge and experience.

Dr. Larkin wrote:

The conviction of Patrick was upon medico-legal evidence alone. It is an outrage that a man's life should have been sworn away by such testimony. In the autopsy on Ferrari we had a man who undeniably died of chloroform poisoning. He was found bound hand and foot. The bottle was there. There had been no other factor. Congestion of the lungs were shown to be not co-extensive. The whole medico-legal testimony in the Patrick case fails.

Physicians in other areas of the country also sent communications. Dr. George Miller, a well-known professor of toxicology in Philadelphia, cited many authorities to show that the medical evidence at the trial had been absolutely contrary to the findings of experienced toxicologists.

The court of appeals finally upheld the conviction by a four-to-three vote. Justice Dennis O'Brien, one of the dissenting judges, stated publicly that he was thoroughly satisfied that Patrick was innocent. The decision meant that Patrick still could be executed for the murder of Rice, but in view of the badly split court and the mass of medical evidence in Patrick's favor, the governor commuted the death sentence to life imprisonment.

The medical evidence was not the only information presented to the higher court. I was asked to give and gave a sworn affidavit containing what Dr. Williams had said to me on the day of the autopsy. A similar affidavit was made by Jim Corrigan, a well-known newspaper reporter who covered police headquarters at that time. On the same day that Dr. Williams told me that Rice had died of old age, he made an almost identical statement to Corrigan.

Patrick's lawyers continued their fight even after the death sentence had been commuted. They regularly petitioned each new governor asking for a pardon, the only legal remedy left. In 1912, Governor Dix studied the evidence and granted Patrick a pardon. In issuing it, he wrote:

"There has always been an air of mystery in this important case. . . . I trust that Mr. Patrick will devote his energies to complete vindication of his declared innocence."

Almost twelve years had passed since Rice had died, and during all that time Patrick had been in prison. He had spent all the money he had and the chance of uncovering any fresh evidence at that late date was almost hopeless. Jones, despite his own testimony that he had killed his employer, had not been prosecuted. He was re-

leased for testifying against Patrick and had disappeared.
Patrick decided it was futile to remain in New York.
He went to Oklahoma, where he became successful in the
oil business, and died there.

Certain aspects of the case have always puzzled me.
First, the $25,000 check. Was it forged? Actually, and
ironically, since it was the check that started the entire
chain of events, this was never really established. Patrick
had been prosecuted by District Attorney Gardiner, the
same prosecutor who was criticized for his handwriting
experts in the Molineux case. Since he was trying Patrick
for murder, he had no need to prove the forgery of the
check and he sidestepped the issue.

Logic dictates against the check having been forged.
Patrick was one of the few persons that Rice seemed to
have trusted. He frequently made out very large checks
payable to Patrick, and the lawyer handled millions of
dollars in securities for him. If Patrick had wanted to
steal from Rice, he could have pocketed the securities or
the large checks made out to him at any time with no legal
recourse by the millionaire. Patrick earned large fees and
had money.

The misspelling on the check is one that an elderly and
ill man easily could have made. If Jones told the truth
when he said he wrote the body of the check, it also is an
error he could have made, since he was not an educated
person. If the check had been forged, then Patrick had to
know it, and he would have examined it with great care
and noticed the mistake in spelling.

According to the story told by Jones, he notified Patrick
after the murder. This makes Patrick's presentation of a
forged check even more illogical. He knew he was the

heir to a ten-million-dollar fortune, and with Rice dead it soon would be his. Why should he have bothered with a paltry $25,000, when he did not even need the money at the time, when simply by waiting for the will to be probated he would collect an amount fantastically higher?

The murder of Rice under the direction of Patrick also made little sense at that time. The millionaire's health had been fading rapidly and he was under the constant attention of a doctor. His expected life span was very short indeed; Patrick knew it and could afford to allow nature to take its course.

Patrick had testified that the earlier will leaving the money to the college had been a temporary legal device because Rice was involved in some litigation which might have embarrassed his estate had he died while it was in progress. The will in Patrick's favor was set aside after his conviction, and the various heirs came to an agreement. The college received a large share and changed its name to honor its unexpected donor.

What about the damaging story told by Jones, the valet? I do not believe his story was credible, except possibly to a prosecutor who wanted to believe him.

Jones suddenly found himself under suspicion. He was a weak-willed, if not weak-minded individual. He told different versions of the murder and later slashed himself with a knife in his cell. The wound was superficial. He even tried to blame the lawyer for that, although Patrick was being held in separate custody.

I doubt that any of the accounts given by Jones were the truth; he could have been persuaded to say anything. If any were, then Patrick was a murderer who should have died in the electric chair. It is possible that Jones,

in a fit of rage at his employer, had held a towel over
Rice's face. In his weakened condition, death would have
come very quickly. If so, then the killer was let go with a
pat on the back. The death of Rice had brought many
heirs and lawyers racing to New York. If Patrick could
be eliminated there was a ten-million-dollar-pie to be
divided. Even the prosecutor seems to have been affected
by the huge amount involved, since he paid such a large
fee to Dr. Williams whose testimony made it possible to
charge that a murder had been committed.

As for me, I believe William Marsh Rice's death was
due to the exact causes stated by his own physician on the
death certificate.

CHAPTER THREE

In Old New York

I AM FORTUNATE IN having lived in New York City during its Golden Age, that wonderful and fantastic fifty-year cycle that stretched from shortly after the close of the Civil War to the start of World War I. It was a time of fabulous people, fabulous growth and fabulous events, and I was more than a bystander.

This was the period of the city's greatest expansion. The first wave of Germans and Irish already had arrived, but now the immigrants came in ever increasing numbers not only from all over Europe but from everywhere in the world, and you literally could see the city growing by convulsive leaps. Stretches of vacant land, once thought too far uptown, vanished almost overnight as the surging population of Manhattan pushed steadily northward from the harbor to the Harlem River, and rookeries sprang up even in back yards on the lower East Side to house the newcomers who were swarming in on boats of every description. The city was luring more than new immigrants; millionaires who wanted to crash society, and farm boys who were yearning to be millionaires, were among the many others swelling the population.

I don't know whether it is great times that produce great men, or great men who produce great times, but the combination of both existed in that fifty-year span. It was during this age that many of the important basic inventions of the modern world were introduced, men amassed fortunes beyond even the dreams of kings, and we saw many of the immortal stars of the theater, the opera and the concert stage. It was a time of magnificent opulence and luxurious living for the rich, stinking poverty for the poor, and yet a period where any man might make a great fortune. And it also was a time of flamboyant characters who might have stepped out of the pages of fiction, yet they were real and I had the good fortune to meet and know many of them. It was a wonderful era in which to grow up, to play and work.

I was a boy of five, wide-eyed with wonder at the sights of New York, when I arrived in this country. While I always have considered myself of French descent, in reality I am a typical American blend. My father was French, my mother was Danish, and I was born on July 27, 1862, on the island of Trinidad in the British West Indies.

My family on both sides had been connected for generations with various of these far-flung dots on the sea. My father was born on Guadeloupe, a French colony. His forefathers, in the late 1700's, had been sent there by the King of France to establish sugar plantations, and one of my ancestors had been appointed governor. My mother

was born on St. Croix, where her grandfather, who had
served as chamberlain to King Frederick VI, was governor
of the Danish islands of St. Croix, St. Thomas and St.
John.

The sugar plantations on Guadeloupe had been worked
by slave labor, and when they revolted in 1848, my father,
then a boy of fourteen, and his sisters were shipped to a
boarding school in this country. Some five years later my
father returned to liquidate what he could of the family
holdings and went to Trinidad, a former French possession, where the family also owned some property. His sisters had remained in this country, he always longed to
return, and so we moved here and he established himself
as a sugar broker with offices at 7 Hanover Place. My
mother's death, when I was seven years old, brought us
into even closer relationship, and my earliest memories are
of visiting my father's offices on Saturdays and school holi-
days and eating lunch at Delmonico's, located then at
the corner of Beaver and South William Streets.

My father's death, when I was fifteen, ended plans for
me to go to France for the final years of my education, and
my guardian sent me to a boarding school in Connecticut.
But after the excitement and gaiety of New York, I found
the bucolic countryside not to my liking and I walked out,
going to live with my grandmother.

By the time I was eighteen I was earning $150 a week,
a large income for those days, and I was a typical dandy
of the period, dressed in a dark cutaway coat, vest and
light trousers, with the inevitable derby hat. Sometimes I
sported a cane. A friend had obtained the exclusive sales
rights to a fine Havana cigar, and we opened an office
on Wall Street and the money poured in. For two years I

led a gay life, attending the theater, the opera and taking part each year in the French Ball held at the old Madison Square Garden. I was no stranger to places along the Bowery and in the Tenderloin. The amusement center was moving uptown from the Bowery, and one of the most popular places was Koster & Bial's Music Garden on Twenty-third Street, just west of Sixth Avenue. It appealed not only to the masses but to the carriage trade as well. Here everyone ate, drank and listened to the music of Rudolph Bial's orchestra. On Saturday nights it was a favorite gathering place for politicians.

Around the corner on Sixth Avenue was the beginning of the burgeoning Tenderloin district with its mammoth dance halls like the Haymarket, Buckingham Hall, and the Star and Garter. Latter-day historians have given the impression that the Haymarket was nothing more than a caterwauling house of prostitution. This is not true, particularly of its early days when it was the finest dance hall in the city, a highly respectable place where young men could bring their girls for a pleasant evening of dancing, or where boys and girls could meet. Rowdies were quickly ejected and so were any ladies of the night who came in hoping to solicit business. No man had to patronize dance halls for that purpose. The side streets of the Tenderloin were overrun with streetwalkers, and red lights burned purposefully over doorways of houses in the district that operated openly with the connivance of graft-collecting police.

The rapid pace at which I was living took its toll, and a doctor thought I had developed tuberculosis. He suggested that I spend the approaching winter in a warmer climate, and I went to Havana where I had relatives.

Upon my return I found that our financial bubble had burst; we had lost our cigar agency, and I decided it was time to plan for a career.

Since that moment when as a young boy I had watched my first torchlight pre-election parade with its noisy brass bands and ringing oratory, I was fascinated by politics. I noticed while playing the role of young man about town that whenever I entered the finer restaurants or cafés, or attended the theater or other expensive entertainments, there would be a generous sprinkling of political figures. They dressed well and lived well, and it was obvious to me that politics offered a splendid opportunity for a young man. I observed further that many lawyers were actively associated with politics, and law had been one of the fields of study my father had discussed with me before his death. His father had been a lawyer. I decided to become active in politics and to study law. Although I didn't know it then, it was this decision that was to lead to my life's work in the coroner's and medical examiner's office.

It was not necessary at that time to attend a law school; you could become a lawyer by studying and working in a law office. A friend introduced me to Nelson Smith, a prominent attorney, whose clients included many large business firms and some of the wealthiest people in New York. He was active in the Democratic organization.

Nelson Smith was a shrewd and good-natured man. He was kindly, too, because he did not even smile when I presented my card with a flourish. I had been christened George Genouillac Petit LeBrun, but I had dropped the plebian-sounding George. The card carried not only the mouth-filling name but also bore a crest of the family coat-of-arms. Later, when I became more active in politics, a friend advised me that my name was too foreign-sounding, and I became plain George P. LeBrun, American.

Mr. Smith agreed to place me in his office. The salary was miniscule, paying little more than my carfare and lunches, but he told me I would have the opportunity of adding to my income by serving legal papers. Through my work with him I met some of the fabled people of that era.

I will never forget my first view of Hetty Green, known as the "Witch of Wall Street," and believed to have been the richest woman in the world. I was in the outer office when a middle-aged woman, accompanied by a plain, sad-looking girl of sixteen, walked in. The woman was wearing an old, faded black dress, a battered straw bonnet, and a pair of worn and unpolished black shoes. A shabby black shawl was draped around her shoulders. Her cheap black cotton gloves had been mended so many times it was difficult to see any of the original material left in the fingers. The girl was wearing an equally rusty black dress. My first thought was that this pair was making the rounds of the building begging for alms. My jaws must have gaped when the woman said, "Young man, tell Mr. Smith that Hetty Green is here to see him."

I hurried into Mr. Smith's office, convinced that we had a madwoman on our hands, but he chuckled after listening to my description of the pair. "That's Hetty and her daughter, all right," he assured me. She was suing a banking firm for $250,000 and Smith was representing her.

I soon learned more about this strange woman. She always approached our office on foot, her head bent low so that nobody could get a clear look at her face, and all the time she was darting quick glances about her. She was suspicious of strangers she saw in the office and had a fear of being trapped by an enterprising newspaperman.

The only thing she ever talked about was money, and she always had a new triumphant story to tell me about how somebody had tried to outdo her but how she had outsmarted the villain. She dealt in millions of dollars, and would walk a mile to save a penny. She hurried in one morning in rare high glee. She had to send one million dollars in securities to Philadelphia to close a deal and had asked the Adams Express Company what they would charge. She discovered that this would be slightly more than the round-trip train fare to the Quaker city, and so she casually tucked this fortune in readily negotiable bonds in her reticule, and took the train herself. She wasted more than five hours of her valuable time, had saved less than one dollar, and was as proud as if she had made over a million dollars, which she did on occasion.

I couldn't help feeling sorry for a poor buggy dealer who thought he could beef up his profit on a sale. The summer heat had forced Hetty to seek relief from her Hoboken apartment, and she rented a room at the Ocean House in Far Rockaway. She came to the reluctant conclusion that she had to have a buggy for use there and marched in and out of second-hand places inspecting the merchandise. She finally found what she wanted in an establishment on Wooster Street, beat the man down to a seventy-dollar price and ordered the buggy delivered to the Ocean House. When delivery was made, she refused to accept it.

"It wasn't the buggy I bought," she told us. "The one they sent me wasn't worth more than thirty-five dollars. When they found out I was Hetty Green they thought I wouldn't know the difference, or that I would come back and buy a more expensive one. I didn't go back. They couldn't cheat me." She paused for a moment and then added casually, "You know, I loaned the Brewsters a half-million dollars on their carriage plant."

If Hetty Green said that the carriage delivered to her wasn't worth more than thirty-five dollars, that was precisely what it was worth, because if she loaned the Brewsters half a million dollars, you can be certain that she knew as much about buggies as the manufacturer did.

I am one of the few people who ever had the opportunity of visiting Hetty Green's Hoboken apartment, and I still have difficulty believing what I saw. Mr. Smith had given me some papers which required her immediate signature and sent me to her home to get it.

When I reached the building I thought I must have jotted down the wrong address. This country's richest woman was living on the top floor of a grimy, dingy walkup tenement where she was paying a rent of twelve dollars a month. I was puffing when I finally reached her door. She would not unbolt the lock until she recognized my voice and even then she only opened the door a crack until she was certain that I was alone.

You entered her apartment directly into the kitchen of a typical four-room railroad flat. We never left the kitchen, which served as her office. She invited me to sit down on a rickety chair while she sat at the kitchen table and carefully read the papers, pen in hand, and occasionally made notes. It took her some twenty minutes to read the documents, and this gave me an opportunity to study my surroundings.

The total furniture in the room consisted of three

kitchen chairs and the table. The floor was covered with oil cloth, there was a coal- and wood-burning stove, an ordinary pail containing coal, and an open wooden stand with shelves holding a few pots and pans and some cracked and chipped dishes. I could hear her daughter moving around in the front room, but she never came into the kitchen. After Hetty had studied the papers and signed them, she placed them in a large envelope, sealed it, and then handed it to me. She shook her finger at me and said, "Young man, be very careful and do not let anyone see this until you deliver it into Mr. Smith's hands." I reassured her and left. I learned later that she was living in New Jersey in order to avoid paying New York taxes.

While Hetty kept piling up her millions and living in little better than a hovel, her husband, a fine-looking man, lived in comparative luxury at the Union Club on an allowance she gave him. I also had to deliver some papers to him.

Mr. Smith finally won his suit for her against the bank. It had been a long and arduous case for him, and his fee of $25,000, considering the work and the amount of money involved, was reasonable. Hetty promptly offered to pay him $20,000. It was not that she thought his fee was excessive, but she liked to haggle and it was almost second nature to her to offer less. She always bought low and sold high. He refused to compromise, and she quarreled bitterly with him but finally paid him in full, a most certain sign that she recognized that his fee was fair, since she was in constant litigation with other lawyers because of her claims that she was being overcharged.

The daughter inherited some of her mother's traits.

When she was in her seventies, she appeared before the surrogate contesting her brother's will. Asked her age by an attorney, she replied, "Put me down as over fifty, young man. And while standing there doing nothing, will you give me your own age and name?" She was the widow of Matthew Astor Wilks of the Astor family.

While Nelson Smith had made no comment about my calling card, he remembered it. He had been engaged as chief counsel in an important suit, and one of the lawyers told him that a process server was unable to break through to serve the necessary papers to C. G. Franklyn, agent for the Cunard Steamship Company. Mr. Franklyn was a prominent society figure who lived in a large private home on Washington Square, at that time one of the finest residential sections of the city.

My employer asked me if I still had any of my cards and when I nodded told me how I could get in to see Mr. Franklyn and serve the papers. "Go up to his house," he directed, "and when the butler opens the door, give him one of those cards of yours with the crest. While Mr. Franklyn doesn't know you, he will think you are a new arrival from abroad, belonging to the French nobility, and I am sure he will see you."

I followed his instructions. The butler took my card, placed it on a small silver plate, and ushered me into the reception room. A short time later Mr. Franklyn entered the room, holding my card in one hand and extending the other, saying, "How do you do." We shook hands. He then invited me to sit down. By this time I was very much embarrassed at having fooled him. I handed him the subpoena. He opened the paper and when he saw the contents, he left the room without saying a word. I found my way to the front door before he could instruct the butler to hurry me out.

Mr. Smith later laughed at my discomfiture. "Your family crest ought to entitle you to a substantial fee," he remarked, and the other lawyer did pay me twenty dollars for serving the paper. Because of this I got a reputation for being able to serve papers, and other lawyers friendly with Smith would get permission to use me. But I only presented my card with the crest just once again, this time to a prominent Wall Street lawyer who knew all the tricks, and it was the only way I could enter his office. The crest again worked like a charm.

Actually, I found that it was not difficult to reach important people, and I even received a tip from Andrew Carnegie when I served him. Mrs. F. B. Thurber, wife of a wealthy merchant, had organized the American Opera Company, and it had failed. The singers and chorus members sued under their contracts. Mr. Smith represented Mrs. Thurber and decided to subpoena the entire board of directors of the opera company, including Mr. Carnegie.

I arrived at his home in the early morning and was admitted without any delay. After I served him and he read the paper, he said, "Young man, I want you to do me a favor. I'm very busy today and can't stand around waiting to be called to the witness stand. So when the lawyer is ready to put me on, will you go to the telephone and call me at this number? I can get to court in fifteen minutes."

I assured him I would and as he was leading me to the door, he reached into his pocket and pressed a five-dollar gold piece in my hand. He laughed when I tried to return it to him. Still thinking I might have compromised the

service of the paper, I hurried back to see Mr. Smith. He
told me to keep it, that it was not a bribe. I did telephone
Mr. Carnegie when it was time for his appearance, and
after he left the stand he sought me out and thanked me.

Even with the occasional extra money earned serving
papers, I was unable to support myself, and the inherit-
ance I had received was dwindling rapidly. I reluctantly
halted my law studies in order to take a better-paying job
and became a cashier and assistant to the owner of the
Albemarle Café at Broadway and Twenty-fourth Street.

During the 1880's this café was a favorite meeting place
for actors, writers and men about town. Delmonico's had
moved to the opposite corner and occupied a building
with entrances on Broadway and Fifth Avenue. The
Madison Square Theatre was just around the corner and
next to the Albemarle was the noted Hoffman House,
headquarters for leading politicians and millionaires. One
of the owners was Edward S. Stokes, who had been released from prison after serving time for the shooting of
Jim Fiske. A feature of the Hoffman House was its huge
oil painting, "Nymphs and Satyr," that would cause any
woman of that era to blush. The free-lunch counter was
presided over by a waiter named Oscar, who frugally
saved the lavish tips he received and became better
known later as Oscar of the Waldorf.

The Albemarle was a lighthearted and cozy place with
a large rug in the rear and four tables with comfortable
chairs that were set apart from the rest of the place. It
was there that I met such famous actors as Maurice
Barrymore, E. H. Sothern, Richard Mansfield, the much-
married Nat Goodwin, and other celebrities and wits.
Clyde Fitch, the playwright, liked to talk to me in French.

One night I entertained a group of the actors by giving an impersonation of Henry Irving singing "It's English You Know," and Maurice Barrymore clapped me on the back and urged me to go on the stage. Instead, when I had saved a little money, I returned for a short time to Smith's office.

I was living at that time in a boarding house on West Thirty-fourth Street operated by friends of mine. The good boarding houses of that era had no relationship to the dreary rooming houses of today. They were run more like private clubs, served excellent food, and employed many servants. They were well furnished, and the guests had free use of the downstairs rooms.

I was a friend of Leon Saxe and his family. He was French, having originally come from the Alsace region. One night I received an urgent invitation to come to see him. A young pianist, sixteen years old, had arrived here with his mother, and Saxe had taken him into his home. I listened to him play and was thrilled by his performance. At my request he agreed to come to my boarding house and play. We arrived after nine o'clock, and the lower part of the house was dark. I opened the Steinway piano and he began to play selections by Chopin. Within moments everybody in the house hurried downstairs, and when he finished they kept begging for more and more encores. The young man was Leopold Godowsky, destined to become one of the world's greatest pianists. That fall when he gave his first recital at Steinway Hall, then on East Fourteenth Street, I went about town placing announcements in hotel lobbies and other places.

He later married Frieda, one of the Saxe daughters, and we continued our friendship until his death. I would

visit him whenever he returned from one of his world
tours. He maintained an apartment at the Ansonia Hotel,
and one night there Mischa Elman, the great violinist,
pointed to Godowsky and said to me, "He is our master."
I was with Godowsky during the tragic death of his son,
Gordon, and later when he lost his beloved wife.

Across the street from the boarding house was the home
and office of Dr. Stephen De Wolfe. On my first visit there
I met his young daughter, Elsie, and when she learned I
was French, she told me she was studying the language,
and always practiced her French on me after that. She
later went on the stage, became a noted decorator and
after her marriage to Lord Mendl became an interna-
tional social figure.

I became active in politics by joining the local Democratic club of my district. When I decided I would have
to leave Mr. Smith's office for a better-paying job, I was
naïve enough to believe that membership in a political
club was a passport to political patronage. Grover Cleveland, a Democrat, had recently taken office as President. I
knew this country maintained an American consul in
French Algiers. I reasoned that there were few Americans
who would want to go to Africa, and since I spoke French
as well as I did English, I was ideally suited for the post.
The fact that I was twenty-two years old at the moment
did not disturb me. I mentioned the thought to Mr.
Smith, and since he believed that experience is a good
teacher, he suggested that I draw up a petition to President Cleveland carefully outlining my qualifications. He
also arranged to have all members of the New York City
congressional delegation sign it.

Now certain in my mind that the appointment was all
but an accomplished fact, I left for Washington and ig-

nored the gloomy forebodings of my congressman who had dutifully arranged an appointment for me at the Executive Mansion, as the White House then was known. It was a hot July day in 1885, and when I entered the President's study he was busy wiping his face with a large white silk handkerchief. He shook hands with me, told me "The French make very good citizens," and suggested that I leave my petition with his secretary. I left elated, returned to New York expecting any day to receive a letter or telegram advising me of my appointment. Two months later newspapers reported the post had been given to a prominent Southerner, and not long after that I went to work at the Albermarle Café.

Although disappointed, I continued my membership in the political club but I found I was not advancing much in politics. I noticed that the men who got the most attention from the important leaders were the heads of political organizations, men who could deliver votes at election time, and so I founded the Franco-American Democratic Club. My reasoning was correct. I soon was introduced to Richard Croker, leader of Tammany Hall, and took an active part in the next city election. The French colony was small and not too many were interested in the politics of any party, so the membership of my organization was not very large. Even so, this taught me an important and fundamental lesson in American politics: You must deliver before you can expect to receive.

Toward the close of Cleveland's term in office, I again was in financial straits and had to abandon for good my apprenticeship in law, but now as a leader of a political organization I merited some consideration. My sights no longer were set as high; frankly, I was willing to take anything. Instead of sunny Algiers, I found myself in the dead of winter taking a train and then a boat to Eastport, Maine, one of the northernmost points in the country. I had been appointed an immigration inspector to enforce the Alien Contract Labor Laws on the Canadian border; salary, five dollars a day.

I was the typical New York politician on my arrival. The ground was covered with snow and it was zero weather; I came ashore wearing a heavy ulster, a silk hat and carrying a cane. I was introduced to my first speakeasy there, some thirty years before national prohibition. Eastport was a dry town, and I had a foretaste of what the future would be like. One of the deputy customs collectors invited me to have a cocktail and I accompanied him down Main Street into what appeared to be a candy store. We entered a back room in which there was a buffet bar stocked with liquor and glasses. Many men were already there and as a newcomer I was introduced to the president of the local bank, the postmaster, the doctor, and most of the leading businessmen of Eastport. On the way out I was told to pick up some peanuts from the show window as a cover-up for our reason for entering the store. I discovered later that it was a futile gesture since only the blind could have failed to notice the existence of the speak-easy. There was one difference, though, from its later counterparts. The liquor was good and uncut; it was brought in openly from across the border.

Just across from Eastport is the island of Campobello. The following summer a resident pointed out a house there as belonging to a fellow New Yorker, James Roosevelt. A boy of seven was playing in front. I was told he was Roosevelt's son, little Franklin. My job in Maine lasted less than two years. Not long after the Republican administration took office, my post was abolished.

As a result of the Lexow Committee which exposed politically-inspired graft and corruption, a movement was started in 1893 to take control of the city government away from Tammany Hall. I owed no allegiance to that organization and felt this was a fine opportunity for a young and ambitious politician to make a name for himself, and I organized the Latin-American Democratic Reform Union, bringing together citizens of French, Spanish and Italian birth or descent.

I was becoming wiser and more astute in politics. Although there were not as many Italians in New York then as today, they still greatly outnumbered the French and Spanish, so it seemed good politics to me to have an Italian as the head of our organization. I invited Antonio Zucca, a respected businessman and a leader of the Italian colony to become our president. The municipal election that year was a bitter campaign. The opposition labeled us the "Hot Tamales."

We supported William L. Strong, a banker and a Republican, and he defeated the Tammany candidate. Because of our efforts we expected some practical recognition and suggested Zucca for the post of one of the four excise commissioners. I visited Mayor Strong on a cold, snowy day shortly after he had taken office. He looked out of the window after greeting me and then remarked, "It's a cold day for an Italian." When I asked him if that meant Zucca was not being appointed, he quickly assured me he was giving it full consideration. The next day he announced his appointments, and Zucca was not named.

Several months later a new law added to the number

of city magistrates. I still thought our group should get recognition. One of our members was John V. Bouvier, Jr., of French descent, a young lawyer associated with a well-known firm. I asked him if I could present his name for appointment as magistrate and he agreed. Once again I was disappointed, but I did become friends with Mr. Bouvier. It was beyond the realm of our imagination that one day his granddaughter would become this country's First Lady, Jacqueline Bouvier Kennedy, the wife of President John F. Kennedy.

It was during Mayor Strong's term in office that I first met Teddy Roosevelt. He had been named president of the board of police commissioners. A young man I knew had taken the civil service examination for patrolman, stood high on the list, but because he had no political connections was never appointed. I met Commissioner Roosevelt and told him about it. He investigated and the very next morning appointed my friend to the force. Every time I saw Mr. Roosevelt after that, including when he was President of the United States, he always inquired as to how my friend was making out on the force. He was delighted to learn that he had risen to lieutenant and had an excellent record.

Although our organization was nominally Democrat, we also disliked the party's choice of William Jennings Bryan for President and supported McKinley. But when the municipal campaign was in the making in 1897, the city Democratic organization asked for our support. This time they were planning to nominate an able man. We had learned a lesson from our experiences with Mayor Strong, that political promises are valueless, and so we were not waiting until after the campaign. I asked for a place on the ticket for Zucca and he was nominated for coroner. After he won the election, Zucca named me secretary to the coroner. He did this on his own without consulting Tammany Hall. Although it was a personal appointment on his part, still it was the fruit of my fourteen years in politics that led me into what was to become my lifetime career. Zucca made one error. His fellow Italians had no objection to my appointment since I had fought for the nomination of the first Italian to a city office, but they rightly expected him to name one of their number as coroner's physician. Instead, he allowed a Tammany leader to dictate this appointment and it probably led to his defeat four years later.

It is a murder case that typifies best many characteristics of the Golden Age; in fact, it is a crime that could have happened only during that era. In it we have a man of enormous wealth, a creative genius, and the naïveté, the opulence and even the decadence that was so much a part of that fifty-year span. The case that mirrored the times so well was the murder of Stanford White by Harry K. Thaw.

Consider the cast of characters and the setting: Thaw was a playboy, an eccentric, and an heir to forty million dollars. White was an architect whose beauty of design helped change the structural face of this country, who created gems of buildings and monuments. The Washington Square arch, the Columbia University library, among many others, are permanent reminders of his genius. He was fifty-two when killed, a man about town, and if the story told by Evelyn Nesbit is true, he was so jaded sexually that he obtained his thrills by pursuing young virgins and ravishing them while they were drugged.

Evelyn Nesbit was the girl, sixteen years old when despoiled, breathtakingly beautiful, and almost country-fresh from a small town in Pennsylvania. She said White gave her a glass of champagne that tasted bitter, the room went black, and when she awakened she found herself naked in bed with White in a room where the walls and even the ceilings were mirrored, reflecting every line and curve of her magnificent figure, a setting reminiscent of Roman orgies even to her blood on the sheets. This trusting girl said she had looked upon Stanford White as a kind, fatherly sort of man who swung her in a red velvet plush swing that was part of the equipment of what newspapers later referred to as his love nest.

The setting of the murder was opening night of a new musical comedy, *Mam'zelle Champagne,* on the roof garden of the beautiful old Madison Square Garden, designed by White. A new show there was an event, with handsomely gowned and bejeweled ladies and men in formal evening wear in attendance. The roof garden was a late supper club where guests sat at tables rather than regular theater seats.

Thaw had recently married Evelyn Nesbit, and she had told him of her seduction several years earlier by White. That night Thaw, Evelyn and two friends attended the opening. White was there seated alone at a table. The Thaw party did not remain very long, and when they arose to leave Thaw lingered behind. He passed White several times and stared at him, but the architect's attention was riveted on the stage. During his final pass of the table, Thaw suddenly pulled a revolver from his pocket and fired three shots directly at the seated man, killing him instantly. While the other guests leaped up in alarm, Thaw broke open the gun, removed the remaining bullets and surrendered to a uniformed fireman on duty at the door.

Not much later on that night of June 25, 1906, I was projected into the case. I was home when I received a telephone call from Coroner Dooley informing me that an important murder had occurred. Although I was not assigned to Dooley, he asked that I work with him. We met in front of the Garden and rode the elevator to the roof.

When we arrived, Thaw and his wife were standing together, surrounded by police officers. White's body was still at the table, slumped in a chair. Thaw freely admitted the murder to us and said, "He ruined my wife." He was quite calm and cool in his behavior. After the shooting his wife had said to him, "Look at the fix you're in now," and he had replied, "I probably saved your life."

Not long after Thaw was taken to the East Thirtieth Street stationhouse and placed in a cell there, I was amused to see Daniel O'Reilly, a former assistant district attorney under Asa Bird Gardiner, hurry in, accompanied by Tod Sloan, the famous jockey. O'Reilly had been having supper at Rector's with Sloan when he heard of the shooting. He quickly grasped the publicity values of the case, to say nothing of the size of the fee that a defense counsel would be able to charge, and he left the restaurant immediately without finishing his meal. He tried his best to talk Thaw into retaining him for the defense, but the prisoner told police to notify his lawyer, Lewis Delafield.

There was a sharp change in Thaw's appearance when he was brought to the coroner's office the next morning. He was pale and agitated; his eyes were bulging and he did not seem to be able to focus them on one person or spot, constantly shifting his gaze around the room. He was perspiring heavily and in the few minutes it took for Coroner Dooley to commit him to the Tombs, and for me to fill out the forms, his handkerchief was drenched.

Former Judge Olcott, who was recommended by Delafield to lead the defense, advised that application be made to the court for a commission to pass on his client's sanity, but neither Thaw's mother nor the son wanted an insanity plea and Olcott withdrew. Thaw wanted his defense to be the so-called Unwritten Law, a novel thought in this instance, since the seduction not only took place long before the marriage but before Thaw even knew the girl.

The defense finally used what was a new approach then, the theory that Thaw was temporarily insane at the time of the crime, but had recovered his reason after it.

Evelyn Nesbit Thaw was the star witness of the case. She told of her horror at waking up in bed and discovering that she had been seduced, and how White had soothed her by saying, "The greatest thing in the world is not to be found out." She related that while she and Thaw had been traveling together in Europe he had proposed to her, but she had turned him down because she feared he would be a laughingstock because of her ruin by White. She had told him how the architect had drugged her with champagne, and she related how it had affected Thaw. Her marriage refusal puzzled me because Thaw hardly could have thought she was chaste. They had been traveling and sleeping together in Europe while he kept proposing.

Some people pointed out that the seduction scene she described was her version and that White was dead and unable to refute it. The presence of the red velvet swing in White's private studio was a fact, and while there may be nothing more innocent than a healthy young girl swinging on an old apple tree under the summer sun, the presence inside a studio of a red velvet swing on which he wanted young girls to swing, does suggest an unhealthy atmosphere.

The first trial ended with the jury hopelessly deadlocked. At the end of the second trial, Thaw was found "not guilty because of insanity at the time of the act." Jerome, who prosecuted, refused to release Thaw and had him committed to the New York State Asylum for the Criminally Insane at Mattewan. There were several lengthy lunacy hearings after that, and Thaw each time was adjudged still insane. He managed to escape and reach Canada, where officials refused to turn him over to New York. Instead, he was dumped into Vermont and managed to reach New Hampshire, where he was arrested. A federal court pronounced him sane and in 1915 a New York jury also said he was sane. He was returned to an institution for another seven years after he was convicted of horsewhipping a boy. He managed to stay out of any further substantial difficulties from his release in 1924 until he died in 1947 in Miami. Evelyn Nesbit divorced Thaw, married her stage partner, divorced him, and slipped into obscurity. Now and then when some momentary interest was revived in the Thaw case she would appear in vaudeville and night clubs, a relic of Old New York.

CHAPTER FOUR

Business as Usual

                       I LEARNED EARLY IN the coroner's office that Big Business had more than a casual interest in our activities, particularly in our inquests. Railroads, public utilities, oil companies, large excavating and building contractors and other firms who employed men doing hazardous work usually had at least one important politician on the payroll, or at their beck and call, to act as a fixer when men were killed on the job.

The large corporations were not concerned with finding out how or why employees were killed; too often they knew only too well that they had failed to apply or enforce reasonable safety measures. They were more interested in making certain that these failures were not attributed to them or that their responsibilities were called to public attention. Corruption became a normal part of their operations. If the fixer could reach a friendly coroner who was amenable to political pressure, he would see to it that the coroner's jury was packed with friends of the company, and a verdict would be brought in saying that the deceased had met death because of his own carelessness. Such verdicts saved money for companies in several ways. Death claims now could be settled for minor amounts, if paid at all, and there was no need for installing costly safety equipment or to hire a sufficient number of supervisory personnel. Where political pressures did not work, these firms were quick to offer bribes or to condone perjury in order to cover up their questionable practices. And let me emphasize that I am speaking here from personal experience.

Commodore Vanderbilt, who founded the New York Central Railroad, has been quoted as saying, "The public be damned." If he did not say it in fact, his successors at the turn of the century seemed to agree with the theory.

At that time the Park Avenue tunnel of the railroad, leading in and out of Grand Central station, was the scene of many mishaps. While the trains ran below street level, most of the Park Avenue trackage still was not roofed over, and the tunnel itself began near Fifty-eighth Street. As a locomotive entered or left the tunnel, belching its usual smoke, the vapors would hit the roof and bounce down in front of the engineer, momentarily obscuring his vision. The trains used soft coal. Trackwalkers were killed and minor collisions occurred, particularly in the two-block stretch of the tunnel from Fifty-eighth to Fifty-sixth Streets, where the steam clouds collected most heavily. Since train service was frequent, particularly during rush hours, the air in this section had little chance to clear before it was fogged up again. In rainy or muggy weather, not at all unusual in New York, the tunnel took even longer to clear.

Some of the signal lights were geared to ring a gong or to explode a torpedo to halt a train that passed a red light, but these seldom could be heard above the noise of the trains clattering through the tunnel. None of these lights had automatic stopping devices. One of the signal lights was fairly close to the entrance inside the tunnel where the smoke was heaviest. After each accident reporters had little difficulty gathering bitter remarks from railroad workers who for years had been protesting the smoky conditions in the tunnel. Railroad officials often issued statements that they were taking steps to correct the situation but that it would take time. New York Central officers could not plead that they were unaware that a hazard existed.

On the morning of January 10, 1902, the inevitable happened. A speeding express entered the tunnel and moments later rammed into the rear of a stalled train. The light was red on the signal inside the tunnel entrance, but Engineer John M. Wisker said that he had not seen it because of the haze in the tunnel. It was a gray day with high humidity, and smoke just clung in the atmosphere. Wisker said the track usually was clear at that time for his express train to conclude its run into the station.

Coroner Gustave Scholer and I left at once for the tunnel. Even now, some sixty years later, I still recall the scene vividly. All available hospitals had sent ambulances with crews of doctors and nurses. The boiler on the express had cascaded live steam, boiling water and flaming coal onto hapless passengers. The stricken locomotive was still pumping additional clouds of smoke into the tunnel and had turned it into pea-soup fog. As we groped our way forward, stretcher bearers would loom up suddenly. Many were carrying motionless blanketed figures. We could hear the screams of the injured echoing and re-echoing underground as they were placed on the roadbed for emergency treatment. The scene had a nightmarish quality of Dante's *Inferno* being brought to life. Eighteen persons were killed in the wreck and dozens of others severely injured, some of them permanently maimed.

Police had been the first to arrive and immediately had arrested Engineer Wisker. After checking the signal light and observing the smoke-filled tunnel, Coroner Scholer told reporters he would hold an inquest six days later to determine the cause of the accident.

A coroner's inquest served an important public function, particularly where the welfare of the people was involved. Although the verdict of a coroner's jury was not necessarily final or binding upon a district attorney in a homicide, it was a different matter when an inquest involved a broad public issue such as safety, health, or working conditions. Such hearings were not cut-and-dried affairs. Testimony frequently was detailed with experts brought in for advice. The findings of such an inquest, particularly where it condemned practices and suggested reforms, was a powerful voice for the common good, and the public usually insisted that these reforms be carried out.

Since Coroner Scholer had indicated clearly that he planned to probe conditions in the tunnel, we knew the New York Central would do everything it could to have

sole responsibility for the accident placed on Engineer
Wisker for passing a signal light, rather than on the railroad's operating policies.

Immediately upon returning to our office we discussed
the selection of a jury for the inquest. As part of my duties
as secretary to the coroner, I had to prepare a list of jurors
to be summoned to sit at an inquest. We decided not to
place on the jury anyone who had any connection with a
railroad, either for or against, and not to accept anybody
recommended to us for service by any politician. We
wanted an unbiased verdict by an honest group of men.

We didn't have to wait long before attempts were made
to pack the jury. Up to then I had always found in trying
to get together a jury that few men seek out such service,
and the more active and prominent a person is, the more
he seeks to evade it and, in fact, will use all the influence
he can to avoid jury duty. The picture changed abruptly
only hours after the train wreck. We were deluged with
telephone calls from busy successful men who suddenly
were anxious to perform their civic duties and were
eagerly offering to serve as jurors at this particular inquest. A retired army general and a former railroad
official were among those who personally hurried to our
office to point out to us their superior qualifications. Perhaps we were unfair in suspecting that all of our callers
did not have the highest motives in offering their services,
but since the possibility existed that some of them might
be prejudiced one way or the other, we politely turned
down their offers.

New pressures now were added. Coroner Scholer was
not the average political hack in office. He had been a
successful physician, interested in good government, and

while nominally a Republican, he had been elected on a reform ticket and was beyond the control of any party boss. I was active in the Democratic party, the head of a political club, but we had demonstrated our political independence on more than one occasion when we refused to back candidates we felt were inferior.

It would be naïve to assume that the New York Central did not have friends in both political parties, and a parade of Republicans and Democrats began to visit us. Some were important, even on the national scene, others wielded county-wide power, and some were lowly ward captains. All had the same story to tell: They realized the importance of this inquest and wanted to make certain that we selected only highly intelligent jurors. By a strange coincidence, all had taken the trouble to jot down the names and addresses of men they would be pleased to see on the jury. By a not so strange coincidence, the same names kept popping up on all these lists. We made it clear to our callers that the names being offered us would not be called for possible service.

Bribery was the final approach. Dr. Scholer was independently wealthy and offering him money simply was out of the question, but I was a wage earner and a prime target. A young attorney I knew only slightly, who was on the legal staff of the railroad, paid me a surprise visit. He said he wanted to talk to me in the strictest confidence and during the conversation deplored what he called the "demagogic" newspaper campaign against the directors of the line. He mentioned that these directors would be offended if the inquest verdict should censure them or the railroad.

By now I had a fairly good idea of what was coming

and I waited quietly. And he didn't wait long either before reaching the point. He suggested that if I placed six men on the jury whose names he would furnish me, men who obviously could be relied upon to make certain that the directors would not be "offended" by the inquest verdict, he would see to it that I was paid $2,500. I have little doubt that this merely was an opening bid and that if I had bargained he was prepared to raise the sum well beyond that figure. I declined his offer without thanks.

For some time after he left, I debated whether to make public his attempt to bribe me. I finally decided to say nothing. My reasoning was simple. He was a young man, only a few years out of school, and held a minor post with the railroad. While he left no doubt in my mind that he was not acting on his own initiative, I knew that the men really responsible for sending him to me would deny it if I talked, and so he would be the only one to suffer. He was nothing more than an errand boy and a cat's-paw in the situation. Perhaps, in retrospect, I should have pretended to go along with him, hoping to trap those responsible, but I doubt if they would have entered the negotiations at any stage, and my initial reaction was anger when I bluntly told him to get out. I might add that as the years passed this lawyer became a vice-president of the New York Central and also served a term as president of the ultrarespectable and conservative Union League Club.

The jury I finally did summon was composed of businessmen from all sections of the city. All were highly respected by their associates and neighbors, and none of them, as far as I could determine, had any ax to grind.

The inquest opened as scheduled, and the jurors were brought to the entrance of the tunnel, where they watched trains enter and leave and observed for themselves the smoke in the tunnel. Coroner Scholer and District Attorney William Travers Jerome questioned some forty-five witnesses, and the inquiry took a week. Among those summoned were the president and other officials of the New York Central. In his closing remarks to the jurors, Jerome told them that if they could find any law under which his office could punish the railroad company and its officials, he would do so.

With an honest jury, the verdict was the only one possible under the circumstances. Engineer Wisker was exonerated and the officials and directors of the New York Central were held responsible. The official findings read in part:

We further find faulty management on the part of the officials of the New York Central and Hudson Railroad, and we hold said officials responsible for the reason that during the last ten years said officials have been repeatedly warned by their locomotive engineers and other employees of the dangerous conditions existing in said tunnel, imperilling the lives of thousands of passengers, and they have failed to remedy said conditions; and also for the reason that certain improvements in the way of both visible and audible signals could have been installed, and the disaster thereby avoided; and for the further reason that no regulation of speed at which trains should be run in said tunnel has been enforced, thereby allowing engineers to exercise their own discretion.

The following day one of the newspapers published photographs of all the directors of the New York Central with a finger pointing to the pictures. The caption under the pointing finger read, "These are the men responsible for the killing of eighteen people."

It is not difficult to understand why the railroad would

have liked to have six men of its own choice on the coroner's jury.

When Jerome placed the case before a grand jury, the engineer became the scapegoat and he was indicted for manslaughter. The same thing has happened before and since in so many railroad accidents that this should cause no particular surprise.

The indictment did have a tragic sequel. Before a date was set for the trial, Wisker's body was found in the Harlem River; he had committed suicide.

It is regrettable that Wisker could not have been tried with competent counsel to defend him. I do not believe that any honest jury would have found him guilty, and it should have been possible to place on the witness stand the same array of railroad officials who had been compelled to appear at the inquest. The coroner's jury found that the engineer could not have seen the signal he passed because of the dense smoke, and I feel certain that any other group of twelve disinterested men would have come to the same conclusion.

But the inquest did have the desired effect. The public was aroused, and the railroad soon found methods of overcoming the hazard.

It would be unfair to pick out just the New York Central, because so many big firms operated on the theory that profits were sacred and that nothing, not even the lives of workers, should interfere. And, of course, there should be no publicity about it.

I received a first-hand lesson in this theory when five men were asphyxiated by toxic fumes while cleaning boats owned by Standard Oil. This was before the oil trust had been broken up into many individual companies.

Soon after the case was reported to our office, I was visited by a prominent politician who, I learned later, was on the payroll of the oil company. He asked me to accompany him to Standard Oil's offices at 26 Broadway, where he assured me I would be furnished with the names of witnesses who could explain how the accident occurred.

I was pleasantly surprised at this offer of co-operation and had visions of a new era dawning. When we reached the headquarters of the oil company, we were brought without any delay into the private office of the secretary of the giant corporation. This official was extremely cordial.

He seemed well prepared for my visit because he was able to tell me in detail how careless these five dead men had been in willfully disobeying company rules and bypassing established safety measures. They had been warned that the disinfectant they were using was dangerous and that they should keep the holds well ventilated. When I sought to learn more about the rules and how the company went about enforcing safety, I learned that it was not company co-operation I was being offered, but rather it was my co-operation that was being sought.

The oil trust in those days was not among the most popular business enterprises with the public and had been receiving some unfavorable mention in the press. The secretary of this vast world-wide business enterprise was not interested in anything as crude as packing a coroner's jury. He knew that an inquest had to be held, and all he wanted was to have it conducted in secrecy, without a jury, if possible, but specifically without any newspaper reporters present. When I pointed out that the coroner's court was public, and secret inquests were held only in rare instances to protect a child, the interview was over.

As we were leaving, the secretary suggested, "Talk to Harry about it."

No bribe was offered and no mention of money was made in the office, but when we were out in the hall, Harry, the politician, again urged me to arrange a secret inquest. "It will be worth your while," he said. By this time I had become so inured to bribes that I didn't even bother answering.

When the inquest was held, the press was well represented. A careless employee must have supplied the secretary of Standard Oil with some wrong information. After the facts had been presented, the coroner's jury returned with a verdict finding the oil company negligent in not providing proper safeguards for the five men asphyxiated. It would seem that they had not been careless after all.

Sometimes business interests resisted making changes even when the amount of money involved was negligible and the improvements suggested were very much to their advantage. I found this true of many real estate firms.

New York began to expand vertically with the introduction of passenger elevators in buildings. As more elevators came into use, deaths in elevator accidents began to rise. Most of the accidents were caused by cars being in motion while passengers were getting on or off. The victims either would slip and fall down the elevator shaft or else get caught between the walls and be crushed beyond recognition.

I was appalled at the mounting toll, because most of these deaths were needless tragedies. There were many inexpensive devices on the market which prevented an elevator from moving up or down until the outer doors were locked. When the Woolworth Building was opened as the tallest building then in the world, the chain store founder told me he had the safest elevators in existence, and he did. He even invited me to witness a safety test of an elevator he had installed in a private house he was having built on Eighty-second Street near Fifth Avenue, opposite his own residence, which he had presented to one of his daughters as a marriage gift. At an additional expense of but twenty-five dollars a car he had installed the latest automatic equipment to prevent cars from moving while doors were open. The average office building at that time had two or three elevators, so for a sum of from fifty to seventy-five dollars or less, the owner of a building could make this improvement. Since a single accident cost many times more than that in legal fees, not to mention damage suits, I anticipated little difficulty in cutting down on elevator deaths.

A survey was made which showed that less than half of the building elevators in the city had safety devices; the others were death traps. The coroners issued a statement advocating the installation of holding devices on elevators. Coroner's juries also called for them after each inquest into an elevator death. Nothing happened and the deaths continued, eighty-five in Manhattan alone in one year.

I spoke to the city building commissioner and urged him to amend the local law requiring the installation of safety devices on elevators. He told me frankly that the real estate firms would run him out of his job if he tried to have such a bill passed. I scoffed, at first, at his attitude until I interviewed some building owners myself and found them almost violently opposed to any such proposal.

Unable to get the city administration to act, I asked
State Senator Sullivan to introduce a bill which would
force action upon the city. The measure was referred to
the senate judiciary committee, and I went to Albany on
the day set for its hearing. On the train I met a lawyer I
knew who told me he had been hired by the Allied Real
Estate Association to fight the bill and kill it in committee. He added that he had ample funds at his disposal.
He won; the bill was not reported out.

It was the death of Supreme Court Justice Bischoff, the
322nd elevator victim in just a few years, that broke the
opposition. There was a shortage of office space in the
courthouse, and the city had rented several floors in a
near-by bank building for judges' chambers. Justice Bischoff had a suite on the thirteenth floor. He had stepped
into an elevator with a companion. When the elevator
stopped at the twelfth floor, his companion saw a friend
and stepped out to talk to him. Just as the car began to
move, Justice Bischoff also decided to get off. He lost his
balance and as the elevator rose, he fell through the open
door down the shaft. I went to the scene with Coroner
James Winterbottom. While we were in the basement
examining the body, reporters from almost every paper
arrived, and I pointed out to them that if the legislature
had passed the bill I suggested, the accident could not
have occurred. They all quoted my remarks. A short time
later the building commissioner publicly urged passage
of the law.

I would like to think that it was my voice that stirred
the action, but I am more inclined to believe that politicians, who do have to visit judges, finally became aware
after Justice Bischoff's death that they were risking their

own lives and stopped supporting the real estate interests in favor of safe elevators.

When it became evident that the bill would be passed, I was offered a different form of bribe. Fast-talking salesmen crowded my office seeking an exclusive endorsement for their particular product, and they painted a rosy picture of handsome commissions for each device sold. They couldn't understand why I turned them down. The best picture for me is contained in the annual reports of the medical examiner's office which now rarely show as many as four deaths a year in elevator accidents in all of New York City.

Happily, too, large industrial firms today no longer consider their workingmen expendable and they have stringent safety programs. But whenever a disaster with many deaths does occur and an inquiry is held, you still will find that the blame is largely attributed to one of the victims. The fixers may still be among us.

Coroners sometimes did keep to themselves information the press would have liked to have, but bribery seldom was involved in these instances. It was rather a desire to protect families from useless scandals.

A prominent New Yorker, and a close friend of Teddy Roosevelt's, left his office late one afternoon to keep a tryst at a hotel with a demimonde of that era. While in bed with her he was stricken with a heart atttack. To the girl's credit, she did not run away but hastily summoned the house physician. The man died before he could be taken to a hospital.

The coroner went to the hotel where he verified that the man had died of a heart attack and there was nothing suspicious about his death. The man's business partner was notified, he arranged to have the body removed to a funeral parlor, and he then notified the wife that her husband had dropped dead while on his way to visit a friend. Newspapers the next morning carried the same story. Neither the wife nor the man's children were told the true circumstances of his death, and since no inquests were held where deaths were due to natural causes, the facts were effectively hushed up.

Justice was neither defeated nor thwarted in this case nor in others of a similar nature as long as the coroner investigated and made certain that death was due to natural causes. The one-day scandal could only have harmed members of the family who were innocent victims. But I always was suspicious when wealthy families tried to exert pressure on the coroner's office when they were the subject of a legitimate inquiry.

I still wonder about the verdict in one case. I can vouch for the absolute honesty of the coroner. I know he resisted tremendous pressure. And yet I still feel that the complete facts were never brought out or examined fully.

Late in the afternoon of November 7, 1907, we received a call at the office from Dr. Joseph Blake, a distinguished surgeon, reporting the death of Charles T. Barney from a gunshot wound. This was sensational news. Barney was a millionaire, a prominent member of society, and newspapers recently had carried reports of a spectacular financial struggle for control of the important Knickerbocker Trust Company. Barney finally had been forced out as president in a battle that had cost him a fortune.

Coroner Julius Harburger and Dr. Philip F. O'Hanlon, the coroner's physician, went to the Barney home at Thirty-eighth Street and Park Avenue. They were met by Mrs. Barney, dry-eyed and icily reserved in manner, who said that a gunshot had been heard in the house at nine-thirty that morning and that it sounded as if it had come from her husband's room. Accompanied by a house guest, she had gone to his room and found him sinking to the floor, both hands pressed to his stomach. A small, five-chambered revolver was on the floor. Mrs. Barney had telephoned Dr. George A. Dixon, who not only was the family physician but also a close personal friend of her husband's.

Dr. Dixon said that upon his arrival he had found his friend in shock and suffering from a severe lose of blood. He stated Barney had told him the shooting was an accident. He had sent at once for Dr. Blake and another surgeon. Both men had performed an immediate exploratory operation and had seen that the wound was fatal. Barney had succumbed at 3:00 P.M.

A short time later Dr. Dixon modified his statement. While with Dr. Blake, he now said, "At no time while we were with Barney did he say a word to us about the shooting." He said it was his personal opinion that the shooting had been accidental.

Harburger also learned that Mrs. Barney had been planning to sue her husband for divorce.

The autopsy was performed by Dr. O'Hanlon, a thoroughly experienced man. He found that the bullet had entered on the left side of the lower abdomen, angled upward through both intestines, continued through the left lung and finally lodged in the muscles of the back, close to the neck, just to the left of the spinal column.

Dr. O'Hanlon wrote in his report:

> I have never, in all my experience of twelve years in examining the bodies of more than a thousand self-killings by shooting, seen one in which the aura of self-attack has been within the space in which was inflicted the wound which caused the death of Mr. Barney. And in all my experiences, I have never known of a right-handed man shooting himself in the lower left abdomen with the muzzle of the pistol pointed upward. That was the only way the bullet could have driven through the larger and smaller intestines.

The autopsy surgeon left no doubt that he did not believe that Barney had committed suicide.

Yet Coroner Harburger, who was not a doctor and who knew little, at best, about gunshot wounds, flatly refused to accept Dr. O'Hanlon's opinion. He insisted that it was obvious that Barney had committed suicide, that he was driven to it by the sudden piling up of his financial and marital difficulties. A reader might say at this point that the fix was in and the coroner wanted to palm the death off as a suicide. I don't believe it. I was present at the conference and I knew Harburger well enough to know that he was sincere when he insisted that it was a suicide.

I know further that Mrs. Barney's lawyer asked Harburger to excuse her from attending the inquest. He refused. "Big Tim" Sullivan, one of the leaders of Tammany Hall, then made the same request. Sullivan seldom asked for a favor; he preferred granting them. In addition, Harburger was his protégé, and the coroner freely admitted that it was Sullivan who had elected him to office, but he was just as firm in turning him down. He said Mrs. Barney would have to testify, and she did. Dr. O'Hanlon gave his autopsy findings at the inquest and told the jurors that since there was no evidence that anyone had shot Barney, the wound must have been accidental.

Harburger, though, was determined upon suicide and in his charge to the jurors virtually ordered them to bring in such a verdict, and they complied.

That was the official end to the Barney case, but there is additional information to be considered. Dr. Dixon filed a claim of $24,000 against the estate for his services. Following customary procedure, the surrogate's court directed him to furnish a bill of particulars itemizing his services to substantiate the claim. Rather than make public the services he had performed for Barney, the physician relinquished the entire claim. According to Mrs. Barney's statement, she found her husband shot at 9:30 A.M., but the coroner's office was not notified until late afternoon. This was a violation of the law requiring the coroner to be notified before a victim's death in such cases, so that an ante-mortem statement might be obtained.

Reporters learned that Mrs. Barney had planned to file her divorce suit in New York. Adultery was and still is the only grounds for divorce in the state. No attempt was made to find out if there was another woman. I heard rumors later that Barney was not shot in his own home but at the home of a married woman and was brought to his own place to avoid a scandal.

Harburger was sincere when he believed that Barney's financial and domestic difficulties pointed to suicide, but he overlooked the fact that these also can be motives for murder. Whether Barney deliberately shot himself, whether he accidentally shot himself at home or elsewhere, whether somebody accidentally shot him, or whether he was murdered, are questions the inquest never resolved. Time also has failed to provide any answer. If there had been no attempt to apply political pressure, I probably would have dismissed it from my mind.

CHAPTER FIVE

Retribution

ONCE A MAN HAS passed his ninetieth birthday, he can be sure the press will take more than a passive interest in each new milestone. Days before each birthday reporters and photographers visit me. By and large, they ask the same questions they have been asking for years and snapping the same kind of photographs. And since I divide my time between Florida and New York, I go through this process twice a year. I worked with newspapermen all during my thirty-six years in office and had many friends among them, so I do not mind. A new note was introduced several years ago when some reporters, with the uproar over the Caryl Chessman execution in mind, began to ask me questions about capital punishment.

This is a difficult question for me to answer. I spent many years fighting for laws to help save lives. I was active in an organization that was founded to help save would-be suicides. I saw innocent men convicted and saved from execution and I discuss elsewhere the possibility of a man who might have been innocent being electrocuted. Every instinct within me cries out against the needless waste of a human life. And yet I recall a case where I thought the death penalty was deserved, and have no reason to change my mind.

There is a vast difference between the teen-age girl of today and her counterpart in the early years of the century, particularly the girls from poorer homes. Few of them then had opportunities for schooling beyond the elementary grade levels, and job opportunities were scarcer; most of them were condemned to dreary lives working in cheerless factories.

The picture brightened somewhat about 1910, the year of this particular case. Girls were beginning to find opportunities to work in offices, and families hopefully scraped together funds to send bright daughters to business school where they could learn typewriting and stenography. The girls were more naïve then and so, I might add, were the directors of some of these schools.

Ruth Wheeler, sixteen and pretty, was such a girl. She was attending a secretarial school hoping for a career in an office. A bright student, she was highly regarded by her teachers, and when the school received a handwritten postcard signed "Albert Wolter," asking for a girl to be sent to him to work as a stenographer at seven dollars a week, Ruth was selected. The card was turned over to her without any checking by the school, even though a business firm would be expected to use its own letterhead.

She left home the morning of March 25, 1910, eagerly looking forward to her first job. Late that night the girl's mother and an older sister, Pearl, entered the East Sixty-seventh Street stationhouse and reported to Captain Edward B. Hughes that Ruth had failed to come home. Usually police are not concerned unless a girl that age is missing for at least twenty-four hours, but Captain Hughes knew the type of hard-working respectable family the Wheelers represented, and he listened attentively to their story.

Mrs. Wheeler explained that after supper, when Ruth did not appear, she decided to search for her, accompanied by Pearl and a neighbor. Another daughter and an uncle remained at home in case Ruth returned while they were out. They became frightened when they reached the address on the postcard, 224 East Seventy-fifth Street. It was a shabby, four-story walkup apartment house, not the kind of place where a man would be employing a stenographer, a fact that a sheltered girl like Ruth, unfamiliar with the business world, would not realize. Pearl told her mother and family friend to wait outside while she went into the building. She learned that Wolter lived in an apartment on the third floor and knocked on the door.

She said that a rosy-cheeked young man, with exceptionally large hands for his size, opened the door. There was a girl in the room with him. The young man invited her in and told her he was Wolter. He turned the key in the lock after she entered. When she asked him about her sister, Wolter laughed and told her he did not know her sister and had not seen her. She said she became frightened at the calculating way he was examining her and she asked him to open the door, but he laughed again and told her not to be in a hurry. The quick-thinking girl then told him that there was a policeman waiting for her downstairs. Wolter promptly unlocked the door and let her go.

Captain Hughes did not like the sound of the story. At that period white slavers were still active in New York, and he suspected that Ruth Wheeler might have fallen into such a trap. He ordered a young patrolman to accompany the Wheelers back to the apartment and make a search.

Wolter was in his pajamas and yawning when Mrs. Wheeler, Pearl and the patrolman arrived. The group looked around the apartment and found no trace of Ruth or any indication that she had been there. At one point, while the patrolman was questioning Wolter, who repeated that he knew nothing about Ruth Wheeler and had never seen her, Mrs. Wheeler moved close to a boarded fireplace. Pearl noticed that it was freshly painted and warned her mother to be careful not to smudge her skirt.

An alarm was sent out for the missing girl. She had been wearing a dark coat and skirt, a white shirtwaist and a double strand of turquoise beads, and had carried an umbrella.

The following morning, still worried about the case, Captain Hughes sent several detectives to the apartment. A young woman was tidying up the rooms. She told them that she did not know where Wolter was. The officers left, waited for the girl to come out and then followed her to a tenement on East 105th Street. When they entered the girl's apartment, they also found Wolter there. Pearl Wheeler had furnished an accurate description of him. He was a good-looking youth, eighteen years old, pink-cheeked, golden-haired, and with unusually large hands.

The officers found a notebook belonging to Wolter in this apartment. In it were the first names of several girls, including a Ruth, with a notation in German script that she had been hired for seven dollars a week. Wolter was taken to the precinct and questioned but he repeated that he knew nothing of the missing Ruth Wheeler. He was held for investigation while police returned to his apartment and once again searched it and found nothing.

The next day, on Saturday afternoon, Mrs. John Taggart, who lived in the building adjacent to Wolter's and shared the same rear fire escape with his apartment, told her husband that he should complain to the people across the court because they had left the fire escape littered with trash. She remarked that she had awakened at eleven-thirty Thursday night, gone to the kitchen for a drink, and noticed somebody shoving a big bundle out on the fire escape.

Mr. Taggart was a man of action. He raised the window and pushed the trash bundle off the fire escape. The couple watched it tumble three stories to the back yard below. Moments later Mrs. Taggart screamed and her husband hurried down the stairs for police. When the bundle hit the ground it had partly opened, disclosing a human head.

A short time later I went to the scene with Coroner Holzhauer and Dr. O'Hanlon. We took the bundle to the local precinct, where we opened it and found that it cointained the partially burned body of a girl. A length of three-eighths-inch rope still was knotted around her neck. The greater part of her arms and legs had been burned away. The head was thrown back and the girl's tongue was clenched between her teeth, suggesting her death agony. Later medical examination showed that the victim had been raped, and soot in the bronchial tubes was evidence that she still had been alive when placed in the fire. The forearms and leg bones above the knees had been broken, evidently so the body could be doubled up to go into the fire. The rope around her neck held in place several turquoise beads from a broken necklace. The victim was identified as Ruth Wheeler.

When we visited Wolter's apartment and removed the freshly painted board from under the mantel, it became painfully clear where Ruth Wheeler had died. The fireplace was a tiny iron affair, two feet wide, two feet high and less than two feet deep. The trussed-up body just about fitted into it. The police officers, who had made the earlier two searches, had never bothered to look behind the board. When the ashes in the fireplace were sifted, officers recovered a hatpin, steel from corset bones, an unburned piece of white shirtwaist, and portions of human bones. The kitchen stove, which also had not been searched, was stuffed with pieces of Ruth's clothing and her shoes.

It was easy enough to reconstruct the crime. Ruth must have been seized and attacked shortly after she had reached the apartment. After choking and raping her, the killer used his large hands to snap her arms and legs, bound the body with wire, and stuffed it into the fireplace. He saturated her with kerosene and fired the body on a bed of charcoal. The girl had been alive all this time. It was a particularly brutal and callous murder.

When he discovered later that the body had not been entirely consumed—it is much more difficult to burn a body completely than people realize—he wrapped what remained in bags and placed it on the fire escape. The body was there when Mrs. Wheeler, Pearl and the young officer made their ineffectual search the night of the murder. It was still there the next day when police again made a search. Fortunately, police are better trained today and do not overlook fireplaces, stoves and fire escapes.

The police and the prosecutor felt they had a strong case of circumstantial evidence against Albert Wolter, but since they knew from past experiences that juries are reluctant to convict on circumstantial evidence alone, they pressed the eighteen-year-old youth for a confession. Wolter calmly insisted that he was innocent and promptly laid the blame on a third person. Every investigator becomes familiar with these stories where it always is a mysterious stranger or friend who really did it. Yet because they contain a note of plausibility, police must check such stories thoroughly, and they often are effective with juries.

In Wolter's case he said it must have been his friend, Frank Abner, who was responsible. He still said he never had seen Ruth Wheeler. According to Wolter, Abner was a German waiter whom he had met in Coney Island. He did not know where Abner lived. His story was that he and Abner had planned to start a business school and he was going to teach German shorthand. The two of them had sent cards to a number of business schools asking for graduates. They had wanted the girls to teach in the school they were going to start.

On the day of the murder he had lent his apartment to Abner and did not know what had happened during his absence.

Although police did not believe Wolter's story about Abner, they knew that if the defense could produce a single witness who had ever met or seen him, Wolter never would be convicted. Detectives began a long and thorough search for the mysterious friend. Some visited agencies who handled the employment of waiters. Others asked hundreds of German waiters if they knew or had heard of a Frank Abner. Every restaurant in Coney Island was canvassed. The description of Frank Abner, furnished by Wolter, was printed in all the newspapers. Police were unable to locate a single German waiter with that name, or one who matched the description furnished by Wolter.

Slight additional circumstantial evidence was turned up. A salesclerk identified Wolter as having bought a brush and a small can of black paint on the day of the murder. Wolter admitted the purchase but denied having painted the fireplace board and suggested that Abner must have done it.

The coroner's office also was working on its own phase of the case. Dr. George S. Huntington, professor of anatomy at the College of Physicians and Surgeons, was asked to help reconstruct the mutilated body from the various charred fragments we had.

The iron nerve of the youthful suspect broke just once before the trial. Katchen Muller, the girl who had been in the apartment with him, sent him a letter. It was turned over to him unopened. He read the enclosed note and fainted. It was written in German, and police quickly had it translated. It read:

"My dear Al: As you have been good to me, I beg you to tell the truth. They found a sack on your fire escape, and from what they tell me I think you are guilty. I beg you to tell all. I will

forgive you. You have been so goodhearted to me I can scarcely
believe it. Take my advice and tell everything. You know what I
know. I appreciate your kindness, but I believe you guilty, and
I beg of you to confess, and no matter what happens I will love
you. Katie."

Feeling that the break was at hand, police questioned
Wolter when he revived, but he still insisted he was innocent. He explained he had fainted from the shock of
learning that his girl had doubts about him.

Wolter's father at first agreed that his son must be
guilty. He said he had been what we now call a problem
child. The boy had left home at an early age and although
he had held no known job, had managed to get along.
But as Wolter continued to insist that he was innocent,
his father changed his mind and retained W. D. Scott, a
prominent criminal lawyer, to defend him. It was Scott,
incidentally, who had married Blanche Cheseborough
after he helped her get her divorce from Roland Molineux.

Public sympathy also began to build up for the golden-
haired, rosy-cheeked youth with the innocent, boyish
face. A wealthy woman, who remained anonymous, gave
money for the defense. Although it was believed to have
been Mrs. John Murray Mitchell of Tuxedo Park, her secretary denied it. Mrs. Mitchell was silent. Wolter's parents
began receiving cards of sympathy from strangers in
which they berated the police and the district attorney
for trying to railroad an innocent boy.

The trial started off in an atmosphere of hysteria.
Women of all ages stormed the courtroom for a glimpse
of Wolter. His photograph had been published in the
papers and his angelic appearance stirred at least the

maternal instincts of these women. We are more familiar
with these orgiastic manifestations today where bobby
soxers and mature women seem to lose emotional control
at the sight of singing stars and movie idols, but it was
a new experience in 1910.

The prosecution quietly went ahead presenting its
case. Katchen Muller was placed on the stand. The girl,
who had written to Wolter, "You have been so goodhearted to me," was given an opportunity to explain.
In a low and reluctant voice she admitted she had supported Wolter from her meager earnings as a salesgirl
in a confectionery store. She had to leave her job when
she found she was pregnant with his child. On the night
of the murder she had slept with Wolter in his Seventy-
fifth Street apartment. The charred corpse was then out
on the fire escape. If he were guilty, he had raped a girl
earlier that day.

Police furnished details of their long search for Abner
without finding a single trace that any such person existed.

Then Dr. Huntington took the stand. We in the coroner's office had been looking forward to this moment.
The anatomy expert said he had examined the remains
of the body found in and near the Wolter apartment.
He had made a study of the color and texture of the
hair of the victim from strands adhering to the scalp
and from fragments found in the fireplace. He held up
one of the fragments and showed the jury that the girl's
hair had been dark auburn. He testified that the girl's
left hand had been tightly clenched and he demonstrated
what he meant.

"You have produced what you say is the remnant of
a hand?"

"Yes, sir; there are some hairs attached to it."

"Were there any marks of fire on the hairs?"

"Only on the protuding portions of the hair."

Dr. Huntington then produced the left hand of the girl, still clenched as he had first seen it. There were singed edges of hair in the fist that appeared to be black. Dr. Huntington explained that he had articulated the bones so that the clenched fist could be opened. He slowly opened the hand, and ten strands of the singed hair came into view. The unburned portions were a bright lemon yellow, the exact shade of Wolter's blond hair. He had described the mysterious Frank Abner as having dark hair.

Wolter was found guilty of first-degree murder.

When he was brought into court for sentence the following month, only a handful of women were in the court and none displayed any sympathy to the still pink-cheeked prisoner. Before passing sentence, Judge Warren W. Foster told the prisoner:

"The crime for which you have been convicted attracted the attention of the whole world, and by its very enormity caused many to doubt your sanity. I have carefully observed you and your conduct in court during the entire week of the trial, and I have detected nothing whatsoever to indicate that you are not sane under the law.

"In addition, I instructed Dr. Maguire, the Tombs' physician, to make a special examination of you, and also requested that a distinguished scientist be present during the trial to serve you.

"The impressions of Dr. Maguire and Dr. Tracy, which will be filed with the papers in your case, confirm my impression that you are morally and legally responsible for the crime whereof you are charged, and of which you have been convicted. It now only remains for the court to impose its final judgment of death."

While being taken to Sing Sing, Wolter showed detectives a letter he had received from Katchen Muller in which the girl asked if he could marry her in prison for the sake of their unborn child.

"I'll marry her if they'll let me," he remarked. "It's due her and I feel very kindly toward her. Poor girl."

"Don't you feel sorry for Ruth Wheeler?" he was asked.

"Of course I do. I feel sorry for her, and for her family. But I am innocent and this will be proved. Abner will be found. I have given a full description of him to the police. Plenty of money has been supplied."

Abner was never found. Not from that day to this. Although hundreds of columns of newspaper space were devoted to the case, not only in New York but throughout the country and abroad, no one ever came forward to say that he knew or had heard of a Frank Abner, a German waiter who once worked in Coney Island.

An appeal for a new trial was denied and so was Katie Muller's plea for a wedding ring.

Albert Wolter became the youngest person, at that time, to die in the electric chair.

Perhaps you would not have voted to convict if you had been on the Wolter jury. Perhaps you believe there was a Frank Abner.

As for me, I believe that Albert Wolter was a sadistic, cruel killer who would have murdered other girls if he had not been caught at that time. Since that afternoon when in a dingy police station I helped open the sack containing the ravished and abused body of Ruth Wheeler, I have felt that Wolter received his just punishment. Time has not mellowed my feelings about this case. I still feel so today.

CHAPTER SIX

"There Oughta Be a Law"

FIVE SHOTS FIRED BY A maniac caused me to become the father of the Sullivan Law, "1897," as it is known to law enforcement officials. More than fifty years have passed now since Section 1897 of the penal law was enacted and New York became the first state with effective means of clamping down on the indiscriminate purchase of firearms. No one disputes today that Section 1897 has been of tremendous usefulness, yet only a few states have followed suit with really efficient laws. Public indifference or ignorance, plus the rapacious greed of a small group of men, still gives the underworld a free pass to plunder, rob and kill.

It was on the morning of January 23, 1911, that David Graham Phillips, a talented writer who had earned both critical acclaim and popular applause, was shot down as he was about to enter The Players Club in the Gramercy Park section of the city. Witnesses had noticed a man loitering about the entrance for some time. When Phillips approached, this man yanked a pistol out of his pocket, pumped five shots into the writer and then, turning the weapon upon himself, sent the sixth shot crashing into his own brain.

The dead assassin was Fitzhugh Coyle Goldsborough, thirty years old, a member of the Harvard class of 1901, a composer and an accomplished violinist. He was a descendant of one of the oldest families in Virginia and Maryland.

Although the two men lived near each other, Phillips did not know Goldsborough, had never met him, and there was no reason why the demented man should have had any grievance against the author. Yet the shooting was deliberate; Goldsborough had taken the trouble to learn that Phillips made a daily visit to his club, where he usually had lunch, and had lain in wait for him.

While being rushed to the hospital, Phillips recalled that he had received several anonymous threatening letters. He had dismissed them as either from a crackpot or from a friend with a macabre sense of humor.

"I could fight two wounds, but not five," he said in the ambulance. "I guess the odds against me are too great." Those were his last words.

There was little that we could do in the coroner's office. Both men were dead. A notebook found in Goldsborough's pockets contained many incoherent entries, indicating that he had been mentally unbalanced. One notation read, "I deem Mr. Phillips an enemy to society and a personal enemy to myself." Perhaps it is fortunate that Goldsborough turned the pistol on himself and had not escaped, because his notebook indicated that he had

compiled a lengthy list of public figures he disliked, including Theodore Roosevelt, of whom he wrote: "An
example of evolution from Politics to Barbarism."

At the inquest we learned that only a few hours before
the shooting Goldsborough had bought the revolver he
used. He picked it up in a pawnshop for a few dollars.
There had been no difficulty. He simply walked in,
selected the weapon he wanted, paid for it and walked
out. Anybody, man, woman or child, could have done
the same: there were no laws and no restrictions at that
time on the sale of deadly firearms. A section of Park
Row was lined with pawnshops whose windows displayed
a wide variety of guns priced from three to six dollars.
I recall one on display that also had a hidden knife, offering its fortunate owner a choice of how to kill. The pawnbrokers, naturally, featured the firearms as defensive
weapons.

Although I knew Phillips only slightly, I was deeply
shocked by his senseless death. He had many productive
years ahead of him and might have reached the greatness
and brilliance critics were predicting for him and thus
enriched our literature.

For some time I had been disturbed by this free and
easy access by anybody to firearms. On more than one
occasion I had investigated a suicide where a man, dis-
traught by a sudden business reverse, had dashed into a
pawnshop, even swapping his watch for a pistol, gone
to the nearest alley and shot himself. Had these men
taken time to think, to calm down, they could have called
on friends or relatives to tide them over and, in many
instances, these setbacks would have been of a temporary
nature. Even more importantly, if firearms were not so

readily available, they would have had time to think things over. When I asked some of these dealers why they had sold guns to men in such obviously distressed condition, they simply shrugged and remarked that it wasn't their business what a customer did with a weapon; they only sold them. I can't say I approved their callous attitude.

I checked our office figures for the year just ended. In Manhattan, Brooklyn and the Bronx there had been 177 murders by firearms in 1910. Inquiring further at police headquarters, I learned that less than half of the killers had been caught, but what was even more disturbing was the information that during the year there also had been 912 arrests for carrying concealed weapons, mainly pistols. We all know that arrests in any category represent only a small number of the actual offenders. This meant that there were many thousands of armed men roaming the streets of the city. Firearms were available not only to respectable citizens but to the criminal element and the mentally disturbed. While there was a law against carrying concealed weapons, it wasn't worth the ink used to print it since it did not prevent anybody from buying firearms. And it was only a minor violation, a misdemeanor, if you were caught.

To me, it seemed that the law in existence was a perfect example of attacking a problem backwards. The law should have prevented the easy purchase of firearms rather than slightly slap a man on the wrist for carrying a pistol around. We had progressed a long way since our frontier days. There were no hostile Indians lurking behind trees in Manhattan, or anywhere else at that time, and even the Wild West days now were over. With law and order operating everywhere, there just was no logical reason for an ordinary man to walk about armed. I reasoned that the time had come to have legislation passed that would prevent the sale of pistols to irresponsible persons. In the vernacular of that day, "There oughta be a law."

My first step was to sound out the political possibilities, and I consulted Timothy D. (Big Tim) Sullivan, a state senator, a district leader and one of the power bosses of Tammany Hall. If he approved, I knew that the entire city delegation would fall in line and also that many upstate Republicans, out of their affection for Big Tim, would vote for the bill. Sullivan was a colorful political figure who was idolized along the Bowery and the lower East Side, where he was also known as the "Big Fella." It has been said, and never disputed, that he had the largest personal following of any political leader in the history of the city.

Sullivan was surprisingly enthusiastic about my thought. At first he wanted to amend the penal code to make it a felony to carry a pistol without a permit. I pointed out to him that this still would not prevent criminals, those bent on suicide, and the insane from buying weapons anyway. He then told me to draft a bill I liked and he would introduce it.

While Sullivan's personal reasons for wanting the law did not exactly coincide with mine, they were logical and cogent. The lower East Side then was the headquarters for many of the infamous gangs of the city. There were constant fights among them for control of specific territory with many murders resulting from these gang wars. Neither the police nor the public cared very much, as long as gangsters were killing each other, but far too often innocent bystanders got in the way and also were killed.

"I'll do anything to stop those shootings by gangsters," Sullivan told me. "It's terrible when an innocent person gets killed. Everybody runs to me and they want me to have the cops do something, as if the police weren't busy with it anyway. But even when gangsters kill each other I still have troubles. If the police make an arrest, the friends and relatives come knocking on my door for me to get a lawyer or arrange bail. And they're hardly out of the door when the relatives of the victim come to me for a contribution to pay for his burial."

Big politicians, it seems, also have their problems.

Even though I now had Sullivan's backing, experience had taught me that I needed public support as well to make certain the bill would pass. I had no illusions that my name would mean much to newspaper editors if I issued an appeal for such a law; the story, if used, would probably wind up back among the classified ads.

I sat down and wrote personal letters to twenty prominent men, known and respected by the public for their interest in the welfare of the people. My list included John D. Rockefeller Jr., John Wanamaker, Nathan Straus, Hudson Maxim, the inventor, Jacob Schiff, the banker, Dr. Simon Baruch, the father of Bernard Baruch, Bishop Grier, among others.

All of them promptly agreed to serve on a committee, and the first meeting was held on February 14, 1911, only three weeks after Phillips had been killed. I outlined the bill I had in mind and told them that if such a law had been in force then, the insane musician could not

have bought the pistol he used to kill the writer. The bill
would require that any person buying a pocket-sized gun
would have to have a permit, and this permit would be
issued by the police department. Since police themselves
often were the targets of armed gunmen, I knew they
would investigate thoroughly any applicant for a pistol
permit. The bill also provided that dealers in firearms
would have to be licensed, that each weapon would have
to be registered, that a sale could be made only upon
presentation of a permit, and accurate records would
have to be kept so the purchase of any gun could be
traced. The committee approved and we formed the
Legislation League for the Conservation of Human Life.
I was named secretary.

The opposition I expected began soon after Senator
Sullivan introduced the bill. It came from three main
sources—the arms manufacturers, the hardware dealers,
most of whom handled firearms, and the pawnbrokers.
There are times when a pawnbroker can be a necessity;
there are other occasions when, to my untutored eye, he
appears more of a necessary evil, but the opposition of a
small but vociferous group of them against the bill was
pure evil. It was not the loss of the sale of a few pistols
that was bothering this particular group, but a scheme
that was netting them very much more.

Known criminals had found a way to avoid any embarrassing search by a police officer. Rather than carry
their guns around with them, they had developed the
habit of keeping them permanently in pawn. When they
were ready to commit a crime, they redeemed their guns,
and as soon as it was over hurried back to rid themselves
of the weapons. If it was "hot," had been used in a

shooting, the obliging pawnbroker would bury it in his vault for them while baffled police searched elsewhere for the weapon. The busier a criminal, the more often he was paying his redemption fees, which made it a profitable business for the pawnbrokers. Some of them kept open nights to accommodate their nocturnal customers. Other criminals did not even bother owning firearms. They would "buy" a pistol from the pawnbroker for the job and then go through the motions of pawning it when the job was finished, counting the difference in what they paid and received as part of the overhead of conducting their business. In reality, these pawnbrokers were running an arsenal business for the underworld, supplying them with weapons for a good rental fee for a few hours. Not all pawnbrokers, of course, engaged in such shady practices.

To offset this opposition, I enlisted the support of all the criminal court judges and the district attorney and they came out solidly in favor of the bill. In addition, the members of the citizens' committee now went to work, and some of them visited newspaper publishers and editors and others wrote letters urging approval of the proposed legislation. The leading newspapers in the city, the *Times,* the *Sun,* the *Herald,* and the Hearst newspapers, all carried editorials supporting the measure.

When the senate codes committee held a public hearing, I appeared and spoke in favor of the bill. The only opponents present were representatives of the pistol manufacturers and the pawnbrokers. Many of the hardware dealers had dropped out of the fight; some of them had been robbery victims and they were in favor of the bill. Those among them who wanted to handle firearms had no objections to being licensed. The senate committee voted to present the bill.

When Big Tim Sullivan said he would work for the measure, he meant it and made what was for him almost a supreme sacrifice. Although he had served for years in both the state assembly and the senate, and as a congressman in Washington, he rarely ever spoke out on the floor for or against a measure. He preferred to work quietly in the background. Even the official biography he had furnished the *Congressional Record* was in keeping with his desire to remain mute. It was the shortest ever printed and read in its entirety: "Timothy D. Sullivan, Democrat of New York."

But Big Tim announced he would take the floor and speak out for the bill that bears his name. Members of the assembly deserted their branch to come over and listen to Sullivan make a speech. While it may not meet the approval of language purists, his listeners knew it came from his heart, and it deserves being printed. Here is what he told his attentive audience, including a packed gallery:

"Last Saturday night, there was a couple of gangs fighting on the street. A mother with a baby in her arms came along and was shot dead. That, alone, ought to pass this bill. No, I ain't alone in wanting to pass this little measure. There's a lot of other people in the city. Here's a little list. There's the City Club, and District Attorney Whitman, and Police Commissioner Cropsey, and the American Museum of Safety, and Jacob H. Schiff, and Henry Clews, and Isaac Seligman and Rockefeller—" Sullivan paused here, grinned and then added in a stage whisper, "That's John D. Junior, a social acquaintance of mine." His next few words were lost in the sound of laughter. ". . . and there's Judge Foster and the judges of every criminal court in the city. Then there's Nathan Straus. I suppose, maybe, that man stands for good, eh? Down my way, they think he almost stands in the footsteps of the Man who came on earth two thousand years ago, because of what he's done for the poor. This is a bill against murder. I don't know much about the Bible except what I've heard Brother Brackett parlaying on me for the last twenty-four years—and that's so much I feel as I'd read the whole book. But if this bill passes it will do more to carry out that commandment, 'Thou shalt not kill,' and save more souls than all the talk of all the ministers and priests in the state for the next ten years."

Sullivan sat down to a roaring ovation for the longest speech he had ever delivered to a legislative body. Five minutes later the senate passed the bill with only five dissenting votes. It also was passed by the assembly, signed by the governor and became the law.

Encouraged by this action, our committee now tried to get similar legislation passed in adjacent states, hoping to cut off the flow of guns to the underworld, but the arms manufacturers now were thoroughly alarmed and began an active campaign wherever such bills were introduced. Massachusetts passed a watered-down version which I do not think is as effective.

In 1925, Franklin D. Roosevelt organized the National Crime Commission and asked me to serve on a committee to draft model legislation along the lines of the Sullivan Law to be introduced in all state legislatures. No state accepted the bill with all its restrictions against the easy purchase of firearms, a few passed weakened measures that leave large loopholes, and guns still may be purchased in many states with little more trouble than in buying a package of cigarettes. The pistol makers and the small-town hardware merchants in these states are still resisting any efforts to protect the lives of innocent people.

Whether these merchants realize it or not, they are serving as a pipeline in furnishing guns to the criminal element of the country. Quite often when police find guns on gangsters the identifying serial number has been filed down. This leads many people to believe that the guns have been stolen and the numbers erased to prevent identification. Police science today, through chemicals and photography, can restore these numbers, and quite often it turns out that these guns were purchased originally in a state with ineffective laws or none against acquiring firearms. Many such guns were not stolen; the underworld was trying to hide its source of supply. The merchants are honest, they sincerely believe they are making a legitimate sale, but they are so blinded by the dollar bill in their hands that they fail to realize the implications of the sale. The pistol which killed Arnold Rothstein, the notorious gambler, was traced to Minnesota, but the trail ended there because there was no effective law. Had there been such a law, police could have learned who bought the weapon and perhaps this murder might have been solved.

When Mayor Cermak of Chicago was fatally shot by an assassin who intended the bullet for President-elect Roosevelt, the killer told police that he had purchased the gun in a Miami pawnshop for eight dollars. It is difficult to balance a few dollars' profit against a human life.

The cry raised most frequently against legislation to curtail the purchase of firearms is that it violates the Constitution, which guarantees everybody the right to bear arms. The Sullivan Law does not restrict the purchase of rifles and shotguns which are used for hunting, nor does it prevent a reputable citizen who needs a gun from obtaining a permit. It is aimed specifically at keeping small pocket-size pistols from the hands of men who would use them to shoot down human prey. The constitutionality of the Sullivan Law was upheld many times by the court of appeals, and the American Bar Association, after the passage of the law, endorsed it as a sound and salutary measure.

If I had my way, I would have the law be even more restrictive. I do not think it is wise for permits to be issued to anybody outside of law enforcement officials and guards. In my own experience, I saw many storekeepers who obtained permits and bought guns to protect themselves against holdups. When I saw them, they were dead, beaten to the draw by the bandit who already had his hand on the trigger. I would advise store owners to investigate the cost of robbery insurance. It may not be as expensive as they think. Guns are not cheap either. An insurance policy can be canceled when a business is sold; nothing can restore a life when an owner leaves it in a morgue wagon. Each year there are many tragedies in homes where pistol permits were granted; a couple will quarrel and because there is a gun at hand, a shot will be fired; or the exploring fingers of a child will find a gun hidden in a drawer or closet, and the tragic aftermath is a familiar story to any newspaper reader. Even

adults can accidentally wreck their lives when there is a
gun at hand. A few years ago the wife of a prominent
social figure awoke in her Long Island home, thought
she heard a prowler and shot at a figure. She killed her
husband, who, unable to sleep, was walking around in
the dark.

The campaign to get the Sullivan Law passed in New
York had taken only a few months. I now turned to another problem that I optimistically thought would be
far simpler, the mounting number of automobile deaths.

I doubt that any present-day reader objects to the fact
that he must pass an examination in order to obtain a
license to operate a motor vehicle. He knows that it offers
double protection to himself and his family in keeping
incompetent drivers off the road. In fact, there is a movement now under way for periodic re-examination of
drivers to make certain that they maintain a standard of
skills.

But at that time only professional chauffeurs had to
be licensed in New York. Anybody else could enter an
automobile showroom, buy a car and drive it out even
if he did not know the difference between a brake and a
gas pedal. There was no control of any kind over private
drivers.

For a time, police automatically arrested the driver
in any accident involving a fatality, and he was released
in one thousand dollars' bail until the inquest. Since, as
part of my work, I was present at all of these inquests,
I was impressed by the testimony of witness after witness
in the various cases saying that drivers not only were
careless but that many of them did not know how to
drive. More than a few testified that they had just bought

the car, received oral instructions that lasted a minute or two from the salesman, and driven off with no actual lessons. Confronted with an emergency, many of them froze behind the wheel and lost control of the car. Pedestrians had to be alert even when walking on the sidewalk. As the accidents continued to rise, the police force was losing so many man-hours in making automatic arrests that they stopped even this slight safety measure and simply handed a summons to the driver to appear at the inquest. Without any license to show, some drivers gave a false name and did not bother to show up at the inquest.

The Legislation League for the Conservation of Human Life, which had been formed to fight for the Sullivan Law, took up the battle against automobile fatalities. We asked for the licensing of all drivers, with revocation or suspension penalties for cause, and also for the establishment of a traffic court and for a bureau where records would be kept. We asked, but nothing happened. In 1914, after more than one hundred school children had been killed the previous year, I appeared before the Federation of Women's Clubs and asked for their support. They gave it and it now meant that eighty thousand women were actively backing the campaign. Certain now that success was in sight, I went to Albany and asked a friendly legislator to introduce a bill. Still nothing happened. Year after year the bill was introduced. Newspapers by now were actively backing the campaign. They began by running lists of names of people killed and injured but soon had to drop that practice because they would have had room for little else. They switched to printing a running box score. Perhaps motorists thought it was a sporting challenge, because the death toll continued to rise and still nothing happened in legislative session after legislative session.

I have one of the box scores at hand. It deals only with New York City automobile accidents and reads: "Killed last year, 1,073. Injured last year, 29,346." Such figures horrified me because it was such a futile waste of lives and senseless maiming of so many people by unlicensed drivers, but apparently the totals caused no qualms to the automobile dealers who were fighting as hard as they could, making regular trips to the state capitol where they wined and dined legislators and convinced them not to pass the bill. It wasn't until 1922, after I made a personal appeal to Governor Alfred E. Smith and he placed the full pressure of his office behind the legislation, that the state finally enacted a law requiring drivers to pass a test and be licensed. The act also established the State Motor Vehicle Bureau. I do not think that the passage of the bill harmed the automobile dealers and I have a faint suspicion that their sales did not decline and the industry wither on the vine after that date.

I shudder whenever I hear anybody speak nostalgically about streetcars and voice a wish that they could be brought back. My campaign to get streetcars replaced by buses in New York took even longer than the one to license motorists. Statistics are dull figures, but sometimes they can illuminate important facts. As part of my work with the coroner's office and the succeeding office of the medical examiner, I kept a close watch on all deaths. It was by breaking down the automobile deaths that I noticed that many more fatalities were occurring on streets with surface lines than on any other. The reason is almost self-evident. Streetcars in New York City ran in the middle of the street. Passengers getting on and off had to step out into the street. Each corner only multiplied the chances for accidents by oncoming vehicles. Buses, which could pull up at the curb, were far safer, and I urged the elimination of the fixed trolley tracks and the substitution of buses. A few brief extracts from newspaper clippings tell the story of futility:

New York Journal, January 24, 1923:

Motor accident fatalities could be set down thirty per cent if surface cars were eliminated and buses substituted, according to George P. LeBrun, secretary of the Chief Medical Examiner's office. For ten years Mr. LeBrun has made a study of traffic accidents in this city.

The last sentence was an oblique reference to the fact that I now had been conducting this same campaign for ten years.

New York Times, January, 1929:

Death by motor vehicles in New York could be cut down from fifty to sixty per cent, if surface cars were eliminated, LeBrun estimates, declaring that few motorcar fatalities occur on Fifth Avenue, where buses are used, despite its enormous traffic. The average of fatalities for the last fifteen years has been four or five cases a year on Fifth Avenue, as compared with forty-one at crossings on Third Avenue in a single year.

It was the same old story, just new death totals, year after year.

Some twenty years after I began my campaign, and after the inexcusable loss of thousands of lives, streetcars finally began to be replaced by buses. I have no nostalgic regrets at their departure.

Our office also had difficulties with manufacturers whose products were poisonous when swallowed. Even though they were not selling their product to be taken internally, they felt that placing the word "poison" on the label or container would be a sure road to bankruptcy. A weak law was passed, and the makers of such products became artful dodgers in masking the fact that the word was there. State Senator James Murtha of upstate New York came to the city to attend a banquet. He was not feeling well and sent a bellboy to a drugstore for a popular headache remedy. The drug clerk made an error and handed over a similarly colored tin container that was a poisonous insect destroyer. The bellboy received his tip and departed.

If Senator Murtha noticed that the tin was not the brand he had requested, he probably reasoned that the druggist was sold out of that make and had given him a substitute. There was nothing about the package to warn the casual user that it contained poison. The trade name was innocuous and gave no indication of its purpose. A short time after taking a teaspoon in water, he became violently ill and sent for the house doctor. He died within an hour or so. I accompanied the corner on the investigation. The tin can containing the poison was a masterpiece of art work and deception. The law required the word "poison" but laid down no rules. The design on the can resembled elaborate filigree, and it took us some fifteen minutes of careful study to find the word "poison" hidden amid the filigree work.

I took the can and showed it to Al Smith, then an

assemblyman, and asked him to prepare a bill requiring the word "poison" to be prominently displayed in large uncluttered type. The sorrowing legislators, who had lost one of their own members, promptly passed the bill.

I do not believe that any of the campaigns I conducted to help save lives has ever placed an unfair burden on a reputable business. The opposition always was based on fear and not clear thinking, and a failure to understand that a human life can be important.

CHAPTER SEVEN

The Lonely Crowd

MY INTEREST IN SAVING lives has led me into many strange byways, so it is not surprising that I am actively associated with the National Save-A-Life League, dedicated to trying to prevent suicides.

Any big city attracts its share of the young and hopeful. The old bromide is that they are seeking fame and fortune. Of course, a good many are, but a surprisingly large number never had or have their sights set that high; the city represents excitement, gaiety, a chance to make a fresh start in new surroundings, something which they thought that the lonely areas or the small towns in which they lived did not provide.

And for some of them, particularly in a place like New York, the city does not answer their dreams; they find they are even lonelier in the crowds than they were in their small places back home where they at least were among friends and relatives. Daily they watch thousands upon thousands of people hurrying to and from work, dashing in and out of subways, racing along the streets. Everybody seems to be going someplace, doing something, and they have nothing but the sanctuary of some small, ill-furnished room. And it is then that their thoughts turn to suicide. What they don't realize is that many of the crowd they see dashing, racing, and hurrying by are just as lonely as they are; New Yorkers just don't seem to slow down; even funeral corteges hurry along.

Defoe seemed to realize this when he made loneliness one of the greatest problems with which Robinson Crusoe had to contend. And since Defoe knew his London well, he may have been drawing freely on his own experiences and observations in that large city.

Loneliness is not the leading cause of suicide in New York, but it is one of the major causes and one of the saddest. Over the thirty-six-year span I was with the coroner's and medical examiner's office, I found that business reverses was the leading cause for suicide among men.

One of the strangest aspects of suicide is that many victims have selected the most painful ways in which to die.

During the Gay Nineties, many people, particularly women, selected carbolic acid. I can't explain it. It is a terrible and agonizing way to die. At that time there were no restrictions whatever upon the sale of this poison, and any pharmacy would sell enough for a dime to kill several people.

Suicide by carbolic acid was intimately associated with one of the worst plague spots of New York's gaslight era; McGurk's saloon on the Bowery. It got so infamous

that it became better known as Suicide Hall. There were
many cesspools that masqueraded as saloons, but Mc-
Gurk's was just about the bottom of the ladder. It was
frequented by the dregs among streetwalkers whose only
chance at plying their trade was to find a newly landed
sailor who had not seen a woman for over a year, and for
some unfathomable reason McGurk's was a favorite place
for many sailors.

McGurk's started on its way to its peculiar fame as
Suicide Hall because of a botched-up job. A prostitute
named "Big Mame" bought some carbolic acid, emptied
the vial into a glass of water and then attempted to down
it in McGurk's. A watching man, suspecting what was
happening, knocked the glass out of her hand. Some of the
liquid spilled on her face, burning her horribly, but he
saved her life. But one of Big Mame's friends was more
successful and the cycle began.

At the coroner's office we became all too familiar with
the routine at Suicide Hall. Some unfortunate girl would
become despondent, she would visit a drugstore con-
veniently located several doors away, return to her table
and swallow the poison.

Then there would be a call for the coroner. He would
arrive, discover that it was another suicide and order the
body sent to the morgue, quite often with a Jane Doe tag.
These women were known by their nicknames; no one
knew their real names.

McGurk never seemed to mind the suicides. Often the
dancing and the drinking would be going on while police
and the coroner were inspecting the body. In fact, as the
evil reputation of the place spread, it became fashionable
for the "swells" from uptown to go slumming and visit

McGurk's. Some of them probably got the thrill they were looking for when some poor unfortunate drank carbolic acid while they were present.

In 1899 there were 238 suicides in which carbolic acid was used; this, of course, was throughout the city and not just at McGurk's. I did help make it difficult for those who wanted to die downing carbolic acid. I called the attention of the board of coroners to the great number of deaths by this easily obtainable poison, and at the urging of the coroners, the city health department finally passed a regulation forbidding the sale of the poison without a doctor's certificate. It is interesting to note that less than a handful of suicides now die each year by drinking carbolic acid.

Until the change-over to natural gas in New York City, illuminating gas was the favorite method of suicides. It was right at hand, and to hurry up the process many would place their heads inside the oven.

Until the Sullivan Law was passed, ending the easy access to fire arms, suicide by shooting was second on the list. We frequently found a pawn ticket for a watch or a piece of jewelry that the suicide had pledged in order to buy the pistol from the same pawnshop.

Few forms of deaths are so terrible as the plunge from a great height, yet this form of suicide has been growing steadily in popularity. Hardly a skyscraper in New York has escaped having its suicides, and special guards are kept on duty on the top of the Empire State Building to prevent jumpers.

A suicide is running from himself and seldom wants to harm anybody else, but the plunge from a height can be dangerous to others. Many pedestrians have died by being

struck by falling bodies. I have seen some plummeting
bodies that have actually made holes in sidewalks and
have smashed through or badly dented the steel tops of
automobiles. About the only thing that can be said for
this form of suicide is that it is rarely unsuccessful.

The stock market crash and the depression aftermath
began one of the worst suicide periods in the city's history. The figures speak for themselves. In 1927, a normal
suicide year in New York, there were 879 such deaths.
The stock market crash occurred in October, 1929. That
year the total suicides had increased to 1,312. There was
a steady climb upward after that, and by 1934 the total
was 1,378. By 1935 we were beginning to pull out of the
depression, and the total declined somewhat to 1,158. I
selected at random a figure from the 1950's and it was
716, showing how prosperous times bring a decline in
such deaths.

One of the most unusual series followed the failure of
an old banking house. Three members of the family
killed themselves within days of each other.

In most instances when wealthy men jumped or fell
from high buildings, the families always insisted that it
was an accident. The marked increase in leaps from tall
buildings began with the stock market crash. Perhaps the
brokers still were playing percentages. It is always difficult
to prove the death was deliberate without the testimony of
eyewitnesses or the presence of a note. Families have more
than just the stigma of suicide to worry about when they
insist upon having it called an accident. Quite often the
dead person carried a substantial amount of life insurance
that had clauses invalidating the policy in case of suicide
but providing double indemnity in case of accidental

death. Where we were uncertain, we would list it as "jumped or fell," and leave it to the insurance companies to battle the families.

Suicides frequently seem to be imitative; the run of carbolic acid deaths indicated that, but there is other proof as well. On many occasions we would find newspaper clippings in pockets or purses describing a similar type of suicide. I recall one case that occurred prior to the Sullivan Law where the wife of a man who had killed himself asked for the gun as a keepsake. We were unsuspecting and gave it to her. She went home and used the same gun on herself. A noted Davis Cup tennis player killed himself, and a few days later another tennis player jumped from the roof of the building where he lived.

Statistics indicate that hotel suicides are now decreasing in New York. For years such deaths were the bane of hotel managers. There is little a hotel can do if a guest checks in and then uses his room to destroy himself. Hotels fear such publicity because it may drive prospective guests away and sometimes it attracts others bent on killing themselves, adding to the hotel's woes. One of the worst-afflicted hotels was the old Grand Union, which was opposite Grand Central station. Every time I entered this hotel with a coroner, Sim Ford, the owner, would comment audibly, profanely and sadly on the topic of why more suicides had to pick his hotel than any other in New York. And there just was no apparent reason. The area was dotted with other hotels just as convenient, just as nicely furnished. Perhaps there was something symbolic in the fact that the entrance to the station, a departure point, could be seen from the rooms facing the street.

Women are less inclined to suicide than men. The most generally accepted reason is that women have more capacity for suffering. I believe a more important reason is that fewer women meet with business reverses, which is still the primary reason for suicides. This picture may change with the steady increase in the number of women executives. The interesting fact that women are becoming the dominant owners of stock in corporations may also alter the statistics in future years.

Most women suicides shy away from the more brutal forms of death, such as using a gun, a knife or a razor; they are more likely to use gas or poison. There has been an increase lately in the number of suicide leaps by women. The changeover in gas and the difficulty in obtaining poison may account for it. Even in suicides women are vain and seldom mar their faces. Sometimes they will use a gun to shoot themselves through the heart, a knife to slash their wrists, but rarely turn the gun on their heads or slash their throats.

My interest in the Save-A-Life League began in the early 1900's when the Reverend Harry Marsh Warren called to see me at the office and explained that he had formed a society for the prevention of suicides. He was planning to make this his life's work and he asked me to notify him of every suicide reported to our office.

His request startled me, and I wondered if I was the butt of a joke. "I'm afraid it will be a little too late for you to render any service to the suicide," I pointed out.

But Dr. Warren was serious. "It might prevent another," he answered. He told me of a case in which he had arrived at the home of a suicide to find the wife very much depressed. Her husband had been ill with an incurable disease and he had taken poison to cease being a burden to her. But the woman felt that there was nothing left in her life and wanted to join her husband in death. The minister spent several hours talking to her and finally convinced her that she should go on living. Since his experience matched that of our office where we knew that some suicides would be followed by others in the same family, I arranged to have him notified of every suicide reported to our office. He made frequent visits to see me after that and reported on the results of the visits he made to the homes. I later became a member of the advisory committee of his league.

Under the coroner system many cases of suicide were kept from the newspapers by political or financial influence. Family physicians often reported such cases but they were not entered on our books until several days later. In that way they escaped the daily attention of reporters. Newsmen always live in the present and never think to look back to notice if there were any additional entries. Some of the coroners were not above accepting bribes to declare suicides as accidents. This was done frequently as a political favor.

When the office changed to the medical examiner system, Dr. Charles Norris put an immediate halt to any such practise. All deaths were handled in a routine, orderly fashion, and the records were always kept in order. He played fair with the press and the public, and no amount of pressure could get him to list a death as an accident where it had been a suicide. Unless there was convincing evidence, he would order a thorough autopsy, and more than a few cases of seeming suicide developed into cases of murder.

Dr. Norris once remarked that every being is a potential suicide. "No one escapes moments of extreme depression, but it's only the borderline person who kills himself. The strong person never does."

If you read biographies of noted persons, you often will find them mention that at some depressed period in their lives they contemplated suicide but they held back and went on to great accomplishments.

Some years ago Dr. Warren issued a leaflet entitled, "Facts Briefly Stated." It is not because I am quoted in one of them that I am reproducing some of it here, but rather because I feel it contains some important and interesting thoughts:

1. Anyone in great trouble minus hope is in great danger, but anyone in great trouble plus hope is safe. The object of this work is to instill hope.

2. We agree with Dr. Frederick L. Hoffman, the statistician, who says, "Suicide more frequently claims the well-to-do, prosperous and well-educated, rather than the unfortunate, the ignorant and the poor."

3. We believe these words of Hon. H. O. Palmer: "A comparatively small number of suicides is attributed to insanity." Also what Dr. Gray says: "In the majority of cases, suicide is committed by persons who are entirely sane."

4. We shall reduce the number of suicides when we reduce the unrestricted sale of poisons, firearms and other implements of torture.

5. A few words spoken at the right time and in the right way will usually inspire courage and hope. Sometimes money is absolutely necessary. We have known of a loan of five dollars to save a life.

6. The general superintendent of Bellevue Hospital says, "Suicides should be reached before they believe that there is nothing

further in life. I think aid or advice would do much to save them."

7. If Dr. Lyman Abbott's words be true, "Suicide solves no problem, ends no experience, brings no possible peace," then we should guard any who are morbid. When Lincoln wrote, "I must die or be better," his friends watched him day and night.

8. Mr. George P. LeBrun is right in saying: "If friends and kin of those ready to surrender would do their full duty, fewer would be ready to leave life where love still spoke, shone, supported and attracted."

A curious fact about suicide is that late Tuesday morning seems to be the zero hour for the jobless. These people see the want ads on Sunday, spend Monday going hopefully from place to place, and then lose hope on Tuesday morning.

The prevention of suicide is a matter to which many thoughtful persons have given their attention. The Salvation Army was the first to develop offices for the purposes of dealing with persons contemplating suicide, and the Save-A-Life League has also been active and successful in this direction.

I know that some people refer scornfully to suicides as misfits, failures, cowards, but many brave people and many successful people have killed themselves in a moment of despair. My own thought is that a person who is interested in others is less likely to commit suicide. And a person who is interested in others can help cheer up somebody who is depressed.

Literature abounds in suicides. Hamlet's great soliloquy is concerned with the subject: "To be or not to be, that is the question."

CHAPTER EIGHT

Mafia Vendetta

THE MAFIA IS NOT NEW in this country. Members of this sinister organization were among the first wave of Italian immigrants who came here well before the turn of the century. And they lost little time in pursuing their familiar practices of ruling by terror and murder. They preyed on their fellow countrymen, bewildered in an alien land, unable to speak the language, and fearful of going to the police. These people submitted to blackmail demands and allowed this small minority to wield enormous power. The braver ones, who attempted to defy the Black Hand, as the Mafia was popularly called then, were tortured and killed as examples to others. Some of the Mafia members also were active in counterfeiting, passing the crude faked money among their own people, and they silenced those who complained.

As a result, the coroner's office in New York found itself

handicapped whenever we had a case involving members of the Mafia. Respectable and hard-working Italians, some of whom I knew personally, would become evasive or refuse to answer questions; they were too terrified to speak out, even to those whom they knew and trusted. I also had difficulty in obtaining a coroner's jury when prisoners were members of the dreaded Mafia. I saved a newspaper clipping from one of our early cases and I have it in front of me now. One paragraph reads:

"All of the sixteen called responded and turned their subpoenas in to Chief Clerk LeBrun today. When they learned, however, that they had been summoned to act as jurors in the Mafia murder mystery, eight of them disappeared and have not since been heard from."

In this particular case, despite brilliant work by Detective Joseph Petrosino, who headed the Italian squad, organized specifically by the police department to combat the Mafia, justice seems to have lost out. The vendetta, though, took over.

Barrels were a common sight on the streets in the early part of this century. Food packaging then was in its infancy, and most staples, like sugar and flour, were shipped in barrels. Storekeepers would dig into the barrel with a scoop and weigh out the exact amount the customer wanted.

For this reason few pedestrians paid any attention to a barrel standing on an East Side corner on the morning of April 13, 1903. A housewife from a near-by tenement, hurrying to a bakery for morning rolls, noticed that an overcoat in fairly good condition was on top of the barrel. On her way back home she passed it again. The coat was still there and obviously had been abandoned by somebody. She mentally ran through a list of members of her family who might use the coat and decided to take a closer look at it. As she lifted up the garment she glanced down into the barrel, and her frightened screams brought people racing out into the street.

Wedged inside the barrel was the jackknifed body of a man with only the top of his head and part of his face visible between his feet. Coroner Scholer and I were just coming on duty when the report came in. Police were holding back the large crowd of curiosity seekers that gathers so quickly in New York, but there was little we could do at the scene; it was obvious that the killing had taken place elsewhere and the barrel dumped at the spot during the night.

Little else was learned at the morgue. When the body was finally worked loose from the barrel, it was found that the man's throat had been cut from ear to ear. Other wounds on his face and head indicated that he might have been beaten senseless before the killer slashed the jugular vein. The victim was about forty years old, wore a mustache, and had pierced ears. I suggested that he might have come from Sicily since it was a custom there for men to wear rings in their ears.

His pockets were empty except for two handkerchiefs; one was a regular man's size, while the other was small and delicately perfumed. The killers had either overlooked or ignored an unusual crucifix the victim wore on a fine silver chain around his neck. Below the cross was a skull and bones. It appeared to be of foreign make and bore a Latin inscription on a scroll. The man's clothes were expensive and he was well dressed except for his shoes, which were old and worn. No labels or identifying

marks were found on his clothes, including his under-
wear. The shoes were of a popular make.

Police considered two theories: the possibility that the
well-dressed victim had been murdered for his money,
even though robbers rarely bother removing identifying
labels from clothing, or else that it had been a love slaying, suggested by the perfumed woman's handkerchief. It
requires considerable strength to cram a doubled-up body
into a barrel, and this indicated that more than one person might have been involved in the murder.

A good description of the murder victim was dis-
tributed to all newspapers, and hundreds of people visited
the morgue, but no one gave any indication of recogniz-
ing the man. His physical characteristics did not match
any on the missing persons' list.

The barrel yielded a possible clue. A code word was
stenciled on the bottom while the number 233 was inked
on the sides. A sugar refinery identified the barrel as part
of a shipment it had made to a wholesaler, who in turn
had sold this particular barrel to a small shop in the Mulberry Bend section, in the heart of Little Italy.

The owner was voluble but offered little information.
One barrel looked just like another to him. He followed
the custom of the neighborhood and placed his empties
outside for anyone to take away without charge. Poor
people usually took them home and broke them up for
kindling wood. He had no idea who might have picked
up that particular barrel. He may have been telling the
truth, but on the other hand police learned that his small,
grubby shop was a gathering place for a gang of counterfeiters, members of the Mafia, who were under surveil-
lance by secret-service agents. If one of these Mafia

members had taken the barrel, the owner would never have dared tell.

The investigation entered a new phase. Since members of the Mafia might be involved, Petrosino was assigned to the case. He was a short, homely man with a pock-marked face, who was absolutely fearless. He had a deep contempt and a bitter hatred for members of outlaw organizations, and took chances that made other members of the police force blanch. Although he received many death threats, he preferred working alone and was adept at simple disguises. He frequently posed as a newly arrived immigrant and would wander into places controlled by his sworn enemies, where exposure would have cost him his life. He spoke fluently all the dialects of his native tongue.

Because of his exploits, he was adored by the mass of Italian immigrants who were honest, hard-working people, and information would be whispered to him that nobody else could possibly receive.

But there was no information this time for Petrosino and no identification of the murder victim. Reasoning that fear still was keeping lips sealed, Petrosino ordered the arrest of all the eleven counterfeiters who had been meeting in the shop where the murder barrel came from. This was the notorious Morello-Lupo-the-Wolf gang. The men had the usual musical-sounding Italian names, but while the arresting officers collected an interesting arsenal of loaded revolvers, knives and stilettos, there was nothing musical about the chorus of protest from the prisoners. Hoping that one of the suspects might betray some knowledge of the crime, Petrosino had all eleven men brought to the mogue where one by one they were led in to view the body. Petto the Ox, a big lumbering man, studied the body closely and then shook his massive head. "Never saw him before," he told the detective.

The placing of the eleven men in custody did serve one purpose for Petrosino. Some tongues loosened a bit, and he learned that many of these men frequently met late at night in a small café owned by Vita LaDuca, one of the arrested men. Morello, the gang leader, operated a spaghetti counter in the rear of this place. On the night before the body had been found, four men had sat at a table in LaDuca's café. Three of the men were Morello, Lupo, and Petto the Ox, but there was no identification of the fourth man. He could have been a relative, a friend, a business associate, or the man found jackknifed inside the sugar barrel. Petrosino's informants either did not know or feigned ignorance.

It was at this point that Petrosino received an anonymous letter warning him to discontinue his investigation. The note implied that the murder had been a vendetta. Usually a vendetta is an "honor" slaying for one of two main reasons, either as punishment for the seduction of a woman member of a household, or to avenge a death or a grievous wrong.

Petrosino shrugged off the letter and its implied death threat to him. He had been stymied in his investigation in the city and decided to try a new tack. Many counterfeiters at that time were convicted on state charges and sent to Sing Sing. Petrosino knew most of these prisoners, having helped send them there. If the dead man had been a member of some counterfeiting gang, it was possible that one of the inmates might recognize him. It was a break in prison monotony for the men Petrosino inter-

viewed, and they welcomed him. He had supplied himself
with bits of news and gossip about their individual neighborhood: the romances, family feuds, descriptions of
decorations at street fiestas, which were important and
highly competitive local events. And during each conversation he displayed a morgue photograph of the murder victim. It was the same story all over again; nobody
recognized the man.

The last prisoner he saw was Giuseppe DiPriema, who
was not even on the detective's original list of prisoners to
be questioned. Although DiPriema was a counterfeiter,
he always had worked alone and was not part of any gang.
Petrosino decided to see him as long as he was at the
prison anyway. He went through the same routine, but
this time there was an instant reaction when he showed
the photograph taken in the morgue.

DiPriema moaned and in a torrent of words explained
that the man was Benedetto Madonia, his brother-in-law.
He demanded to know what had happened, but Petrosino
wanted more information first. He asked for a detailed
description. The prisoner mentioned some old scars, which
had been found on the body during the post-mortem. He
said Madonia's ears had been "run through," meaning
pierced, and he described the crucifix. Asked if his
brother-in-law had worn any other jewelry, the prisoner
said that he always carried a fine gold watch. His sister,
Benedetto's wife, could provide an accurate description
of it. "She loved that watch," he added. Madonia lived
in Buffalo.

Petrosino told the prisoner how the body had been
found in the sugar barrel. DiPriema discounted the perfumed handkerchief. He said it either belonged to his

sister or else had been placed in the victim's pocket to mislead police. "Benedetto was a fine man, a good family man," he said. As Petrosino was leaving, the prisoner grasped the bars of his cell and told the detective, "I get even with who killed him. I swear a vendetta."

Petrosino returned to the city and checked through the possessions taken from the prisoners at the time of their arrest. One was a pawn ticket, dated the same day the murder barrel had been found, but little attention had been paid to it because the ticket showed the loan of one dollar on a watch. It had been found in the pocket of Petto the Ox, the man who had inspected the corpse with so much interest.

The detective hurried to the pawnshop, where he redeemed the ticket. He was given an elaborately engraved gold watch, worth many times more than the single dollar for which it had been pawned. The answer was clear to Petrosino. After the murder Petto had emptied the victim's pockets. Since the watch was a clue to identification, he had taken it, but he did not want it and had dumped it on a pawnbroker simply to get rid of it. Few pawnbrokers at that time supplied police with descriptions of the articles they accepted, and they could sell unredeemed pledges after the short loan period. In that way the watch would disappear.

Mrs. Madonia was brought down from Buffalo and identified the body of her husband. She also recognized the watch.

Petrosino felt that he had a strong case of circumstantial evidence. He brought all eleven prisoners to the coroner's office, and I took his affidavit charging Petto with the murder of Madonia. The other ten men were charged with being accomplices.

Even with the formal arrest, the fear of the Mafia was so strong that I had difficulty getting enough men to serve on the coroner's jury. At the close of the inquest the jury returned with a verdict against Petto. He was indicted by the grand jury, and the other ten men were held as material witnesses.

From various witnesses Petrosino had painstakingly built up his case against Petto the Ox. He learned that Madonia had been a distributor for Morello and had come to New York seeking help to get DiPriema released from Sing Sing. Morello had no interest in DiPriema and had turned him down. Madonia refused to be rebuffed and one night appeared unexpectedly at a secret hideout of the gang. Alarmed at his knowledge and afraid that he might turn them in for refusing to help his brother-in-law, they decided that Madonia had to die. He was wined and dined at LaDuca's café, taken elsewhere and killed. Petrosino was certain that the Ox was the actual killer. It was the custom for the killer to empty the pockets.

By the time the case came up for trial, the Mafia had done its work. Key witnesses had disappeared, others now told different stories, and so the indictment was dismissed and all eleven men were released from the Tombs.

Petto the Ox dropped out of sight. Petrosino kept his ears open and gradually picked up information that the killer had settled in a small town in Pennsylvania, a safe distance from New York and from anyone who might want to avenge the death of Madonia. DiPriema was released from prison and also dropped out of sight.

Several uneventful years passed. Petto lived quietly in

the small town and behaved himself; he had no desire to call any attention to his whereabouts. On the night of October 25, 1905, neighbors saw him sitting outside his home, smoking a pipe, the picture of a man at peace and content with the world. They went to bed. Sometime later Petto the Ox entered the house and prepared for bed.

Neighbors heard a peculiar shrill whistle, noticed the oil lamp blow out and heard his back door creak open. A short time later five shots roared out. They found Petto the Ox dead in front of his darkened home.

The murder of Petto showed clearly the accuracy of Petrosino's solution of the Madonia killing. It was evident that others besides the detective believed that the Ox was the guilty man. And it is more than likely that this conclusion was reached on evidence more direct than that which the detective had been able to obtain. If the guilty one is not paid off in blood, the entire oath of vengeance remains unsatisfied. Other members of the gang met death in various ways, but no one else was unmistakably a vendetta victim.

The Mulberry Bend section provided the coroner's office with additional difficulties because where Little Italy ended, Chinatown began. It was during this same period that the so-called tong wars broke out; actually these were fights between competing factions for control of gambling rights. Although the warring groups liked to use guns, they were notoriously poor shots and they were busy hitting innocent bystanders instead of each other. Some of the arrests by police seemed to have been made out of sheer desperation, with simply no idea of who did the actual shooting. The inquests rarely added any enlightenment. There would be a parade of solemn-faced Chinese to the stand, none of whom ever admitted being able to speak or understand English, and each question and reply had to be translated. The answers could have been written down in advance without going through the formality; no one saw anything, no one knew anything, no one heard anything. When pressed about the sound of gunfire, the answer invariably was that the witness thought it was firecrackers being shot off to celebrate one event or another. Coroner's juries, as confused as police, simply thew up their hands and returned with meaningless open verdicts.

It was the murder of Elsie Sigel, granddaughter of General Franz Sigel, a Civil War hero, that brought about closer co-operation between responsible Chinese merchants and leaders of law enforcement agencies.

Miss Sigel and her mother, along with other socially prominent women, had been active in mission work in Chinatown, seeking to convert the Chinese to Christianity. The young woman was sincerely interested in her work, formed many friendships with her pupils and invited some of them to visit her at her home.

She was last seen alive on the morning of June 9, 1909, when she left her home planning to go to Chinatown. She failed to return that night, but her worried family was relieved the next day when a telegram, signed in her name, arrived from Washington, D.C., stating that she was all right and would be home the next day. Several days passed with no further word from her, and a quiet search was begun. No one had seen her in Washington, and she had not appeared in Chinatown on the day she had disappeared.

Nine days passed. On June 18, Sun Leung, owner of a restaurant on the second floor at 782 Eighth Avenue, notified police that his cousin, Leon Ling, had been missing for a week. Leon was a friend of the missing Miss Sigel. He lived in a room above the restaurant. Detectives forced open his door, and there was a large trunk, tied with cord, in the center of the room. The body of Miss Sigel was in the trunk. She had been strangled with sash cord. Bruises and scratches on her face and body showed she had put up a vigorous fight for her life.

The murder of Miss Sigel shocked Chinatown and the rest of the city. Dozens of letters she had written to Leon Ling and to Chu Gain, owner of a restaurant in Chinatown, were found in Leon's room. The letters indicated that her friendship with these two men had passed beyond any casual pupil-teacher relationship.

Chinatown was no longer uncommunicative. Police were informed that Chong Sing, who occupied the room adjacent to Leon Ling, also had disappeared. Leon was traced from New York to Baltimore and then to Pittsburgh, where he dropped out of sight. He was well educated and preferred to wear American-style clothes, and police believe that he disguised himself in Chinese dress and fled the country.

Chong Sing was found in Amsterdam, New York, and brought back directly to our office. The coroner asked me to sit in on the questioning along with an assistant district attorney. On the train ride back to New York City, Chong had denied to detectives any knowledge of the murder, but he dropped that pretense in our office and answered questions directly in English.

He said that on June 9 he had been in his room when

he heard noises coming from Leon's room next door. "I heard noises like maybe man and woman playing like wrestling on the floor," was the way he described it. "I look into room when I hear noise. Through keyhole I see Leon and girl make like fight or play fight. Leon, he hold her down on bed. Me see blood, me look again in Leon's room. Me see girl lying back in bed with clothes on, then me see Leon begin to pull off girl's clothes and plenty of blood on her face and coming out of her mouth and nose. Me open door and go in room, see the girl lying in bed all covered up. See feet sticking out and hands. Leon go in closet and bring out trunk in middle of floor, open trunk and take everything out and make trunk empty. Leon go in closet and get rope and drop rope on floor. Me go away quick, go downstairs. Afraid of trouble."

He said that Leon later called him back. There was much blood on the floor, and Leon, unaware of what Chong had seen through the keyhole, told him the girl had bitten her lip. She no longer was in sight, and the trunk was closed. He admitted after further questioning that Leon told him the girl was dead and that he had to get rid of her. He told Chong that he was going to ship the trunk to Europe.

Chong said that the night before the murder he and Leon had been guests at a party Miss Sigel had given at her home. Leon drank too much and became boisterous. He believed that the young woman had come to see Leon about his behavior the previous night and to tell him he could not come to her home again. Leon, who had stolen the letters she had written to Chu Gain, and evidently was jealous, thought he was being banished for another reason and strangled her. I have no doubt that Chong told us the truth that day. All efforts to trace Leon in China failed, and he never was brought to trial for the murder.

As a result of this tragedy, the well-meaning women who had been doing missionary work in Chinatown hurriedly dropped their efforts. It was some years later when Chinatown Gertie got religion and joined Tom Noonan, "The Bishop of Chinatown," at the Doyers Street Mission. Gertie had been an alcoholic pickpocket who preyed on tourists visiting Chinatown when she suddenly reformed, stopped drinking, and became an active mission worker. She had little success among the Chinese but was revered by the Bowery derelicts. Today, there are many active mission churches in Chinatown.

CHAPTER NINE

Coroners for Sale

I SAW MANY CORONERS come and go. Some of them were intelligent and dedicated men who worked hard to make the coroner's court a place where facts and justice were of primary importance. When they presided, inquests were truly a "poor man's court." No lawyer was needed, the atmosphere was friendly and informal, witnesses were not frightened or confused by rigid legal procedures, and the truth would emerge. These men were proud of their office, they recognized its importance and they protected its integrity.

A few of the coroners, and let me emphasize that it was only a few, were outrageous crooks who dispensed "justice" for cash. Their only interest in each new case was to discover how they could extort money, and they used the power of their office for blackmail purposes.

The great majority of the coroners I served under were

political party workers who were finally receiving a reward for their faithful services to a political machine or a party boss. Most of these men were personally honest, but while some were adequate in their work, others were ineffectual. Too often their only qualification for the important post was party regularity, and we even had a few men serving as coroner who could just about read and write. Some of these hacks were more concerned with remaining on the public payroll than with working for the public, and they took orders from politicians.

They either were indifferent or looked the other way when juries were packed, and sometimes they allowed their decisions to be dictated to them from behind the scenes. The coroner's office was an important one for a political machine to control. It was a place where a case could be fixed and disposed of early, before public outcry could build up to a point where no politician would dare to interfere.

It can be safely assumed that some of the politicians demanded or accepted bribes for such influence over a coroner, but there were other and more important advantages to control of the coroner's office by a political machine. The court was a place where favors could be done in return for a generous political contribution, where strong-arm thugs, who performed valuable services on Election Day, could be kept free for future duty. More than one killer walked out of the coroner's court because a packed jury solemnly voted that the thug had acted in "self-defense" when he shot or bludgeoned to death an inoffensive and innocent victim.

An alert or vigorous prosecutor could still have presented the same information to a grand jury and obtained an indictment, but quite often the district attorney had been elected on the same political ticket as the coroner, he was subject to the same pressure, and the verdict of the coroner's jury gave him a graceful out in not pressing the case and saved him from sullying his own record. Even where a prosecutor went ahead and obtained an indictment, a skillful defense lawyer could make good use of the coroner's verdict in raising a question of reasonable doubt in the minds of a trial jury.

Although I am discussing a situation that existed in New York City until 1918, when the coroner's office was abolished, the situation still has its application today. The coroner's office still exists in many cities, and the public, particularly at municipal levels, receives the kind of government it deserves. If people abdicate their rights and accept without protest unqualified candidates for office, they should not be surprised if these men are devoted to a political machine rather than to public service.

It is easy enough to say, "Put in reform candidates," but the worst grafter in all the years I was with the coroner's office was Dr. Moses Jackson, who had been elected coroner on a reform ticket. Because a man shouts "crook" at a man in office, it does not necessarily mean that he will be more honest; he may have even bigger and better plans for thieving when he enters office.

Dr. Jackson, who was a physician, also had been active in politics. We didn't have to wait long for him to exhibit his greed and his belief that his election, even though on a reform ticket, had been a mandate to him to graft, not only spelled out in capital letters but in golden letters as well. His greed and stupidity were truly amazing.

He had little idea of the legal powers of his office or

the scope of a coroner's authority, and he made no attempt to find out. He did know that a coroner had the power to make an arrest, and to him anybody with this power was in a position to demand money.

One of his very first cases involved the death of a workman killed by a falling elevator in the B. T. Babbitt Soap Company plant on Washington Street. A cable had snapped and it obviously was an accidental death. That made no difference to Coroner Jackson.

It was the custom then for detectives to telephone a coroner after he had made his investigation and ask him whether he wanted an arrest made. When such a call was made to Dr. Jackson, he told the detective to arrest B. T. Babbitt.

"Mr. Babbitt has been dead for years," the detective told him.

"Well," Jackson directed him, "go out and arrest somebody who owns the building."

Since the building was owned by a corporation, the puzzled detective finally returned with the building superintendent. Dr. Jackson was satisfied. He didn't care who was brought in, he wanted to use the arrest as a lever. He promptly held the man in five thousand dollars' bail pending the inquest. The bail, for an accident case, was unusually high, but Dr. Jackson had his reason. He believed that the high figure would convince soap company officials that he viewed the case seriously. He happily expected them to bribe him.

He had selected the wrong business firm. The company made no such move despite broad hints by Dr. Jackson. He even postponed the inquest several times in order to give them ample opportunity. He finally had to hold the inquest but was determined to get his revenge and obtain a verdict placing the blame on the company for the death of the workman. In his charge to the coroner's jury he said:

"Gentlemen, this elevator was not fit for cattle. This rich company let this poor man ride on it when they knew it was not safe, and you should hold the B. T. Babbit Company responsible for this man's death."

While the jury was out he walked into an office of an associate, where I was seated, and boasted of what he had done. He was certain that the coroner's jury would recommend to the grand jury that criminal charges be filed against the company, and this would serve in the future as an example of his pay-or-else policy. Just then a clerk hurried in to report that the jury had reached a verdict. Jackson eagerly asked what it was, and the clerk replied the jurors had found that the death had been an accident.

Jackson loudly berated the clerk in our presence and shouted, "You son of a gun, you sold me out."

He was convinced that the clerk had accepted a bribe and had fixed the jury. Not only was the clerk an honest and conscientous person, but it was absurd to think anybody would want to fix a jury in a case where the facts pointed so conclusively to an accident. And the soap company was one that had never tried to fix a case.

Dr. Jackson refused to change his viewpoint that every arrest meant graft for someone and if he didn't receive payment, then somebody had cut in on his prerogative. After the Babbitt case he decided he would always deal directly with the principals.

It was this policy and his own greed that led to his

downfall. A woman dying in Jersey City told police there that she had had an abortion performed in New York by a doctor in his office on West Twenty-third Street. The information was passed along to New York City police, who came to our office for information about the medical aspects of the case before arresting the physician.

Jackson was present and when he heard it was an abortion case, he told the officers to make an immediate arrest and bring the doctor before him for arraignment. The detectives pointed out that while it was a police matter, the case was not within the jurisdiction of the coroner's office because the woman had died in another state. Even so, the coroner bulldozed the officers into a hurried arrest and he sat as a committing magistrate. The accused doctor asked that his lawyer be notified.

It was this information that Jackson had been seeking. He went to the lawyer's office and told him that for a thousand dollars he would discharge the doctor when the hearing was held. William Travers Jerome, an honest and fearless man, was district attorney at that time. The lawyer knew that if his client was freed at the inquest, Jerome would have him rearrested. The lawyer pointed out to Jackson that it would be useless to pay the bribe without the guaranteed co-operation of the district attorney's office.

It was no secret that Jerome suspected Jackson of demanding and accepting bribes. Rumors of his activities had spread rapidly. The two men had clashed several times when Jerome had questioned some of Jackson's actions. In fact, Jerome was so suspicious of some of the coroners that he had organized his own homicide bureau, made his own investigations into suspicious deaths and largely ignored the coroners. He once told a reporter that the office should be abolished. The newspaperman, looking for an even better story, repeated Jerome's remarks to Jackson, who retorted:

"That man is a paranoia [sic]. I'm a member of the lunacy commission. He can get my opinion if he comes to me. He's crazy! He has his smart young fellows up there and thinks he can do everything. He wants to abolish everything except his own office and be the whole thing himself."

Jackson's reference to the "smart young fellows" was an unwitting tribute to Jerome's staff. The district attorney had surrounded himself with bright young lawyers, many of them independently wealthy, who were fired with the same zeal for good government as was Jerome.

Under the circumstances, one would think that even Jackson would have thought twice about going to any member of Jerome's staff and offering to cut him in on his bribe. But since he believed that every man was like himself and for sale, Dr. Jackson telephoned Assistant District Attorney Charles Chadwick, who had been assigned to the abortion case, and suggested they lunch together. Chadwick was one of New York's blue bloods, a member of a wealthy and distinguished family. He had been an All-American halfback at Yale, and is one of the school's football greats.

Dr. Jackson, who came from the tenement district of the East Side, suggested to Chadwick during the lunch that he could throw a lot of business his way if he went into private practice. Then, almost as an afterthought, and with the finesse of an elephant, he mentioned the physician who was under arrest.

"I want to discharge the doctor tomorrow when he comes up at the hearing, and his lawyer will give me one thousand dollars," he told his startled luncheon companion. "If you approve it I'll give you two hundred and fifty dollars."

Chadwick said later he almost fell off his chair at the bald and brazen bribery attempt. His office had been seeking to get evidence against Jackson, and here the coroner was offering him such evidence along with the dessert. Chadwick pumped Jackson, got the details of his visit to the lawyer and his demand for money, and then pretended that he would have to think it over. He did not want to alarm Jackson, who might frighten the lawyer for the abortionist into silence.

Chadwick hurried back to his office and told Jerome of the incident. The prosecutor wondered if Jackson was trying to pull his leg and fool him into making a false arrest. He sent for the lawyer named by Jackson, who confirmed that the coroner had demanded a bribe and promised to fix the case. Both the lawyer and Chadwick signed sworn affidavits, and several hours later Jackson was arrested while at his desk in the coroner's office.

When he was brought before Jerome, who accused him of being a grafter, Jackson retorted, "I'm not such a grafter as you." He still clung to his belief that every person sought bribes. He was convicted, sent to prison, and, of course, ousted from the coroner's office.

Oddly, it was another physician who almost equaled Jackson's record for corruption. Both men served on the same board of coroners, which explains Jerome's suspicions of the office. The staff, aware of his search for bribes, gave him the ironic nickname of "Goldy."

Several persons were killed in a dynamite explosion

while the East Side subway was being built. Goldy hurried to the scene with visions of dollar signs dancing
inside his head. But when he got to Park Avenue and
Forty-first Street, the scene of the blast, he found District
Attorney Jerome already there. He promptly dashed
around notifying every police officer he could find that
he was in charge of the case. His great worry was that
Jerome would act first, make an arrest and present the
case directly to a grand jury, so that he would not be able
to hold an inquest. Without bothering to gather any
details he looked around the streets, saw a laborer standing on the corner holding a red warning flag in his hand,
and told police to arrest him and bring him to the coroner's office.

The bewildered flag-holder, who had nothing whatever
to do with the explosion and certainly was in no way
responsible for it, was hustled downtown, and Goldy
began his immediate arraignment. As the proceedings
were under way, District Attorney Jerome, who had
learned of the arrest, hurried into the coroner's court
and objected to any action being taken against the innocent man. The prosecutor got into a heated argument
with the coroner, and one of the latter's clerks struck at
Jerome. The district attorney countered with a left hook
that almost lifted the clerk off his feet. Taking advantage
of the diversion, Goldy held the workman without bail
and committed him to the Tombs, almost all in one
breath. He then banged his gavel, shouted that court was
adjourned and ran out of the room.

A lawyer for the subway contractor promptly went
before a supreme court justice and obtained the release
of the laborer on a writ of habeas corpus. Goldy had

ducked away so rapidly that he did not learn of this development. The next morning he opened the inquest and sent to the Tombs for his prisoner. An officer told him the man wasn't there, that he had been released on the habeas corpus writ.

"What's that?" he asked.

He was convinced that nobody had the right to take his prisoner away and he wanted to issue warrants of arrest for everybody involved, until the city corporation counsel explained to him that a supreme court writ was more potent than an arrest made by a coroner.

I was pleased by the sequel to this incident. Assisted by Jerome, the laborer sued for false arrest. The coroner, who loved money like life itself, had many anguished conferences with his lawyer and finally settled out of court by paying five hundred dollars in cash. The workman was well compensated for being victimized by a rash official.

Later I learned how Goldy had manipulated a case in which a boy had been shot and killed by an off-duty policeman, who was drunk at the time.

At the inquest the jury exonerated the policeman. The coroner had shunted to a side office the key witnesses against the officer and did not call them to the stand. He received one thousand dollars from the patrolman involved. The boy's mother refused to accept the verdict and went to District Attorney Jerome. She supplied the prosecutor with the names of witnesses who saw the officer shoot her son. She did not know of the bribe Goldy had accepted.

Jerome investigated the shooting, and the officer was indicted for manslaughter. While the patrolman was being

held in the Tombs, Goldy sent his clerk to see him, told
him to keep quiet and he would get his money back. The
officer, probably afraid that Jerome also would indict him
for bribery, said nothing and the money was returned to
him. This was one time Goldy was glad to give up money,
since it saved him from going to jail.

I was fortunate that the two men I served as secretary
to the coroner, Antonio Zucca and Dr. Gustave Scholer,
were wealthy and honest men who could not be bribed.
After that I was placed on civil service, and since the
crooked coroners could not control me, they never tried
to involve me in any of their schemes.

Our greatest difficulty was not with crooked coroners
but with a special breed of predatory small-fry lawyers who
infested the old Criminal Courts Building where our office
was located for many years. These lawyers were always
underfoot and many of them literally seemed to have
their offices in their hats. They would borrow pens and
paper and they carried the necessary legal forms in their
pockets. We always kept the stamp drawer securely
locked. If the building's facilities had been kept open all
night, I believe some of them would have made it their
permanent home.

These lawyers preyed upon the foreign-born who had
difficulty understanding the language and were terrified
at being involved with police or courts, a holdover from
experiences in their native lands. Often they were involved in simple accident cases and would have been released after the inquest. The lawyers would solicit them
as they were being brought in as prisoners, extort as much
money as they could for fees and then tell them they
needed additional money "to take care of the coroner,"

assuring them this would win their freedom. This money also would be pocketed by the lawyers. Occasionally one of these prisoners would be held for further action and he then would start shouting that he had paid money to the coroner. In some instances we forced lawyers to return the "bribe" money to the clients. Others would deny they had told the prisoners they had to give the coroner anything, and all we could do was to tell the prisoners to report it to the district attorney's office.

The antics of these lawyers helped destroy the reputation of the coroner's court and it was unfair to the great majority of coroners, who were honest men.

Ambulance-chasing by lawyers was not against the legal code of ethics at that time, and a surprisingly large number of lawyers, who later became well known in the profession and even rose to hold important judicial posts, were active in this practice. All the newspapers maintained reporters in the building and they covered our court and activities as part of their duties. To assist them in their work, we would hang a slip of paper on a hook whenever a coroner went out on a call. This proved to be a valuable tip service for the ambulance-chasers as well. Whenever a disaster occurred, they were at the scene almost as quickly as we were. They would solicit cases while we still were questioning the injured trying to obtain information as to how the accident had occurred.

There was a collision on the Sea Beach railroad returning from the race track at Brighton Beach, and no sooner had the injured arrived at the hospital than a small army of runners tried to crash in. When they were refused admittance into the wards, they wrote letters offering their services to obtain damages from the railroad company. Newspapers later published some of these letters.

They interfered with our work so much at Bellevue that we managed to get hospital officials to issue an order that only relatives could appear at bedsides. One day after this order was issued, we went to the hospital to interview the survivors of a multiple accident. A priest was moving about talking to the patients, and we assumed that he was comforting them. He kept his back to us. I noticed that one of the victims signed a paper given to him by the visitor, and I walked over. The "priest" was a solicitor for a well-known lawyer specializing in negligence cases. He had rented his clothes from a costume company to pose as a man of the cloth and had succeeded in signing up several of the injured before we discovered his identity and had him thrown out.

One of the active negligence-case lawyers was Martin T. Manton, who had a large staff of solicitors including the walking delegate of the Iron Workers Union. This was before the Workmen's Compensation Law was enacted, and whenever an iron worker was injured or killed in an accident on the job, the delegate would bring the case to Manton. The lawyer became wealthy in his practice, later became a federal court judge, was convicted for accepting bribes and was sent to prison.

The New York Bar Association finally called for the outlawing of ambulance-chasing, and a law was passed making it a misdemeanor for anyone to solicit an accident case. Lawyers now can be suspended or disbarred for such practices.

For years I heard rumors that Abe Hummel had influence with our office and I was puzzled by the reports. Hummel and his partner, Howe, were a law team who won many acquittals in notorious murders. Howe was portly and dapper. Hummel was a short, almost deformed man, who operated in the background. It was largely his behind-the-scenes maneuvering, rather than Howe's eloquence, that won so many of their cases. The firm bribed trial jurors, had a staff of professional witnesses who were prepared to offer alibis at a moment's notice, and if clients were wealthy enough, bought off damaging witnesses, sending them out of the state and even out of the country. Hummel took care of such inside matters as developing breach-of-promise suits into a fine blackmail art. Millionaires who liked to play around with chorus girls were encouraged to write letters to these girls, who promptly turned them over to Hummel. He would then inform these men that he was filing suit unless they wished to settle for damages for breaking a poor girl's heart. Since these men could not risk exposure, they paid. Hummel did have a strange code of ethics. He always turned over to these men all their letters and had a small stove in his office where they could watch them go up in flames. He never tried to collect more than once on a case but he sometimes hooked the same millionaire several times with different girls. It was largely as a result of his activities that breach-of-promise suits finally were outlawed in New York.

The firm seldom had matters within our jurisdiction, and I was mystified by the rumors that Hummel fixed cases in our court until one day when I learned how he had collected three thousand dollars by pretending to a client that he had to pay a bribe.

We always made a careful investigation of death by suicide to prevent any cover-up of murder, but after we were satisfied that there was nothing suspicious, we seldom held a public inquest. We usually closed out the case by calling in a relative for a statement.

In this instance a twenty-two-year-old stenographer had poisoned herself. Her mother came to the office and told me that her daughter had killed herself after being seduced by her boss. He had pursued her for some time, taking her out to dinner and the theater, but after she submitted to him, he had dropped her. The disappointed girl, who probably had hoped for marriage, finally told her mother, stayed home from work the next day and drank poison. That ended the case as far as our office was concerned and it was marked closed on our records.

Her employer, who did not know of our custom, was afraid that his involvement with the girl would come out at an inquest and went to Hummel for advice. The lawyer knew how we handled ordinary suicides and sent a clerk to inspect the list of closed cases, a public record open to anybody. The clerk verified that the case was closed. Hummel did not inform the worried businessman of this but told him instead that there was an inquest scheduled but that he could fix it up with the coroner so he would not be called. He said he would have to pay a twenty-five-hundred-dollar bribe to the coroner and had the gall to ask for an additional modest five-hundred-dollar fee for his services. The man paid the three-thousand dollars and left, convinced that he had saved himself from a public scandal. There was no inquest scheduled or planned, the case was completely over as far as our office was concerned, so Hummel simply pocketed all the money he had tricked the man into paying. Later the businessman boasted how he had fixed a case in the coroner's court. One of his listeners told me the story, and I showed my informant the actual records of the case, documenting that it had been closed without an inquest before the businessman ever went to Hummel. In a way, Hummel's gouging of this man was a touch of poetic justice, and I would have liked to see the businessman's face when he learned the actual facts. The law later caught up with Hummel and he went to prison.

But it was such false boasts and misrepresentations that may have led an anonymous letter writer to question the death of Gustave Bauman, the owner of the Biltmore Hotel. I had been a personal friend of Bauman's for some years. He formerly had owned the Holland House at Fifth Avenue and Twenty-ninth Street, and the hotel was a favorite with the carriage trade. Swiss-born, he had been raised in the tradition of innkeeping, and deft service was his hallmark. When Antonio Zucca, who had first appointed me secretary to the coroner, lost his bid for re-election and I thought I would be out of office, Bauman offered me a post as his assistant. I declined when Zucca's successor, Dr. Scholer, asked me to stay on.

Bauman finally realized his dream when he built the Biltmore, still one of New York City's fine hotels. On October 14, 1914, about six months after the hotel had opened, I received an urgent telephone call to come immediately to the Biltmore. I found Bauman dead; he had fallen from the twenty-second floor of the hotel to the Italian Gardens, located on a second-story setback.

I notified Coroner Feinberg, who was a doctor, and we conducted an investigation.

A hotel carpenter, whose shop was on the extension of the twenty-second floor, said Mr. Bauman had visited the shop to discuss alterations he wanted made on the floor below. After Bauman left, the workman saw him leaning over the coping of the roof, looking down into the Italian Gardens. It was then 11:00 A.M. and every morning at that hour the hotel waiters drilled in the gardens to maintain the precision service Bauman demanded of his help. There were no signs of any struggle on the roof, and the other carpenters in the shop had heard no disturbance. Bauman was a stout man and in leaning over the low parapet may have become dizzy and fallen to his death. Coroner Feinberg was satisfied that it was an accident. Before the inquest, rumors spread that Bauman had committed suicide because of a lack of business, but the financial records of the hotel showed that it already was operating in the black. He was a devoted family man. I had seen him just one week before he died, and he had been happy at the success of his new venture. His death was officially ruled an accident.

A short time later the *New York Sun* received an anonymous letter in which the writer claimed that Bauman had been murdered. The writer mentioned no names, although he hinted Bauman had been having marital difficulties. The editor, knowing of my friendship with Bauman, had the letter brought to me. I took reporters to the hotel, where they were able to conduct their own investigation which satisfied them that the death had been accidental. They also established that the report of marital difficulties was without foundation.

That still didn't end the case. As a successful business-man, Bauman had carried a large amount of life insur-ance. The company, using the suicide rumors as a de-fense, refused to make payment. The entire matter was thrashed out again, this time before a trial jury. The verdict was that Bauman's death had been an accident and the policy was paid. The letter writer never came forward nor offered any information to back up his claim of murder.

Some years later, on the occasion of my twenty-fifth anniversary with the office, my colleagues gave me a testimonial dinner, and I was pleased when they selected the Biltmore Hotel.

Graft and corruption can be halted easily in any cor-oner's office. I recommend that candidates for office should be lawyers who can conduct intelligent inquiries. The doctors on the staff should be skilled pathologists who have passed special examinations and they should have tenure placing them beyond any political control. The investigators and other key personnel also should be on civil service. A coroner tempted to take a bribe or fix a case for a political boss would think twice about placing himself in a vulnerable position where there are witnesses able to testify against him.

CHAPTER TEN

The Untold Story

ON THE MORNING OF July 31, 1915, a grafting New York City police lieutenant was electrocuted at Sing Sing Prison. He was not convicted for taking bribes but as the man who had ordered one of the city's most sensational murders. Since then I have received information in confidence that has made me wonder whether the man died in the electric chair for murder, or simply because he was a grafter. It is entirely possible that an innocent man was legally executed. If so, at best it was done because of blind prejudice. At worst, it may have been done to satisfy a consuming political ambition.

Many readers will have guessed that the police lieutenant was Charles Becker, who died for the murder of gambler Herman Rosenthal.

All the principals now are dead and I do not think I am bound any longer by the terms of the confidence.

I feel that honesty and justice require that the full facts should be made known, and I will reveal them here for the first time. I will name my source, and you will be able to judge for yourself the integrity and the knowledge of that person.

During the early morning hours of July 16, 1912, Rosenthal, a well-known gambler, was seated at a table in the dining room of the Hotel Metropole on Forty-third Street, just around the corner from Broadway. He was reading the first editions of the morning newspapers, in which his name was prominently featured. Just two days earlier the *New York World* had published an affidavit by him saying that his silent partner in a gambling house he had operated in an apartment at 104 West Forty-fifth Street had been Lieutenant Becker, the head of special police squad number one, popularly known as the "Strong Arm Squad," which was specifically detailed to suppress gambling. The next day he told the same story to District Attorney Charles S. Whitman, made an appearance before the grand jury, and was due for another.

Rosenthal was bitter because Becker had raided his place in April. The gambler claimed it was supposed to have been a courtesy raid, made during off hours when no gambling was going on. He was out at the time, but his young nephew and an employee were arrested, and a patrolman was stationed in front of the door thereafter to prevent him from reopening for business.

The Metropole was a favorite meeting place for gamblers and the sporting crowd. From time to time, as he read the papers, Rosenthal read aloud to others items from the news stories to justify his actions to them, since gamblers, traditionally, never talk about their connections with police.

About two o'clock that morning Louis "Bridgie" Webber, another gambler, entered the room, circulated around the tables, paused to speak briefly with Rosenthal, and then left. A short time later Rosenthal tossed a dollar bill on the table to pay for an eighty-cent check and walked out. As he came through the Forty-third Street door, a witness saw a man signal, several other men went up to Rosenthal, and four shots were fired. One tore away part of his skull. Rosenthal fell to the sidewalk and died almost instantly. A prediction he had made only some thirty-six hours earlier, when he had signed the affidavit, had come true. He had said at that time, "I am signing my death warrant."

After the shooting the gunmen ran to a gray Packard parked about one hundred feet up the street, and the car roared east and turned on Sixth Avenue. An actor, Charles Gallagher, made a note of the license plate number of the fleeing car and gave it to police. Other witnesses supplied other numbers, but the actor had been correct. The plate number had been issued to Louis Libby, who operated a limousine service. He said his partner, William Shapiro, had the car out that night. The car was found later in a Washington Square garage where the owner said Shapiro had brought it in after 2:00 A.M. but had requested him to say he had parked it at midnight.

District Attorney Whitman was notified of the murder and went immediately to the West Forty-seventh Street stationhouse where the body had been taken.

Let's pause for a moment to examine a few facts.

Rosenthal's affidavit against Becker already had been published in the newspapers and was in the possession of the district attorney. Whitman had said publicly that he needed more than Rosenthal's unsupported word to act against the police lieutenant. If anything happened to Rosenthal, Becker would be the first suspect; even a dolt could understand that, and Becker had had sufficient intelligence to pass two civil service examinations for promotion. He knew Rosenthal already had done everything against him that he could, and as a police officer he was well aware that legally proving graft is a difficult matter. And Becker most certainly knew that if anything happened to Rosenthal he would be in a much more difficult situation.

When Whitman met reporters shortly after the murder, he indicated clearly that without any information at all as yet, he already had prejudged the case and made up his mind. He told them: "The big thing in this case is not the death of Rosenthal, but the death of public confidence in our system of justice that the murder has gone a long way toward causing. Now the big thing is to take those steps necessary to restore this confidence and to prove that Russian methods of disposing of those who cross the path of the police system can only be employed at dangerous cost." The latter part of his statement was an obvious reference to Becker and it was treated so by the press.

Whitman was an ambitious man. He had sought the nomination for district attorney as part of a long-range plan. With the publicity available to a crusading prosecutor he hoped to win a reputation that would put him in the governor's chair and eventually lead him to the

Presidency of the United States; he was no shrinking violet in keeping quiet about his ambitions.

I applaud any ambitious man, and the nation has gained considerably from such men. Thomas E. Dewey followed the identical route and was twice the candidate of his party for the Presidency. Earl Warren rose from prosecutor in California to governor of his state and finally became chief justice of the United States Supreme Court. But ambition must never interfere with the proper course of justice.

Shapiro was found quickly and he was able to supply officials with four names. He said the car had been hired from him for the night by Baldy Jack Rose, who despite his sweet-smelling name was an unsavory character well known to police. He was a one-time white slaver, a professional gambler, a stool pigeon, and as he testified later, he was bag man or collector for Becker. Because of some early illness, Rose was completely hairless and his skull resembled a billiard ball. His correct name was Jacob Rosenzweig. Shapiro said he drove Rose and Harry Vallon and Sam Schepps, two small-time gamblers, from Tom Sharkey's saloon on East Fourteenth Street far uptown and then to Bridgie Webber's gambling place at Forty-second Street and Sixth Avenue. Later he had driven some of these men to the vicinity of the Metropole. After the shooting the four actual gunmen had jumped into his car and ordered him to drive under the threat of death. He had dropped them off near Bridgie Webber's place. He did not know the identity of the four gunmen but said one of them was the man Rose had picked up uptown.

Police were unable to find Rose, but Webber was arrested. He denied Shapiro's story. He also was an unsavory person whose activities had included running an opium den in Chinatown and conducting stuss games, poker games and gambling houses. He was a business rival of Rosenthal's, and the two men were known to be enemies. Sometime before the murder Webber had been waylaid by several gangsters and given a severe beating. Webber at the time had stated openly that Rosenthal was responsible for the attack on him.

Two days after the murder Rose walked into police headquarters and surrendered, remarking that he heard the authorities were looking for him. His first story gave officials little more than they already had. Two other men who had been seen at Bridgie Webber's place the night of the murder were also arrested. They were Sam Paul, who had made threats against Rosenthal, and Jack Sullivan, "King of the newsboys."

On July 23, one week after the murder, Vallon surrendered. Sam Schepps still was missing. Whitman now had six men under arrest for complicity, one being sought, and none of them apparently the actual gunmen. The known facts indicated that Rose had hired the car, had assembled the gunmen and had conferred all along the way with Bridgie Webber. Taking part in some of their activities were their two henchmen, Vallon and Schepps. Webber was a known enemy of Rosenthal, a man with a motive for the murder, and the fact that he had spoken to Rosenthal at the Metropole and the gambler had then left the hotel and walked into the ambush indicated that Webber had lured him to his death. Despite Whitman's prediction on the night of the murder, he had found nothing to associate Becker with

the murder, although there were ample indications that
the police lieutenant was taking graft. He lived in a
luxurious home, far beyond the income of his school-
teacher wife and himself, and he had a large amount of
money deposited in banks. A fall-out among gamblers
is not of much interest to the public; it is not the stuff
that makes headlines or a hero, as would the prosecution
of a renegade police official.

A brief inquest hearing was held on July 24 by our
office. Whitman did not want any of the men in custody
questioned, and Becker was not summoned. Of the few
witnesses called, a barber and a waiter made the case even
bleaker against Rose, Webber, Vallon and the missing
Schepps when they testified that they saw Webber running
away from the Metropole immediately after the shooting
of Rosenthal. The waiter said Webber had given the
signal to the gunmen.

Shortly after the inquest District Attorney Whitman
announced that he had obtained confessions from Rose,
Webber and Vallon. The three men had placed the
blame on Becker. Rose said that Becker had ordered him
to hire the gunmen and kill Rosenthal because he was
talking. The bald prisoner said he had kept delaying,
but Becker had issued an ultimatum on the same day
that Rosenthal saw Whitman and demanded that it be
done that night. He said Becker threatened to frame them
unless they carried out the execution. Rose's story was
confirmed by Webber and Vallon.

Rose also furnished the names of the four gunmen.
They were members of "Big Jack" Zelig's mob on the
lower East Side. Their aliases have enriched criminal
history. They were Frank Muller, alias "Whitey Lewis";

Louis Rosenberg, alias "Lefty Louie"; Harry Horowitz, alias "Gyp the Blood"; and Frank Cirofici, alias "Dago Frank." Their names were withheld temporarily while police could round them up.

Whitman called a night meeting of a grand jury, and Becker was promptly indicted for first-degree murder. The prosecutor also revealed that in return for the confessions he had given a written guarantee of immunity from prosecution for murder to Rose, Webber and Vallon, provided that none of them had fired any of the actual shots which killed Rosenthal. In other words, in return for their testimony that they had arranged the murder on the orders of Becker, they would go completely free despite their complicity in the crime.

When Becker was arrested he denied all knowledge of the murder. He claimed that Rose had acted for him as a stool pigeon in obtaining information about gambling places. He also denied taking graft which, of course, greatly weakened his denial of the murder. Becker said that on the night Rosenthal was shot he had gone to a newspaper office to return some clippings he had borrowed from a reporter, then had attended the prize fights at Madison Square Garden and had gone home. His first knowledge of the murder, he said, came from Frederick Harley, a reporter, who had telephoned him after the shooting. Rose, in his confession, said he had notified Becker after the shooting and said the lieutenant told him he had heard about it and congratulated him.

There still was a vital flaw in Whitman's case against Becker. The common law under which we operate is the result of many hundreds of years of experience. And from this experience has come the rule that a prisoner cannot

be convicted solely upon the testimony of an accomplice,
that independent corroboration is needed. It is fairly
obvious that a man trying to save his own neck will
readily try to shunt the blame upon somebody else,
whether that somebody else is guilty or not. And the
story told by Rose, Webber and Vallon made them accomplices. Independent corroboration was needed.

Whitman did not have to search for such corroboration. His three prisoners, who had lengthy conferences
with their attorneys before they confessed, were able to
supply it. It was none other than the missing Sam
Schepps. All four of them had gone to a conference with
Becker in Harlem, where he was planning to raid a gambling house. They had met in a vacant lot, and Becker
had told them that Rosenthal had to be killed. Schepps,
however, had not taken part in the conference. He had
remained at the curb talking to the chauffeur who had
driven the car, so he was not in on the conspiracy and
therefore was not an accomplice, but yet could testify
to the conference taking place and so corroborate the
story. The date of the conference was indefinite.

Further, Schepps was not really missing. Rose and his
attorney knew where he was all the time, in Hot Springs,
Arkansas. Now Schepps hurried back to New York and
supplied the vital missing link.

The case was complete against Becker and he could
be placed on trial. Defense attorneys objected to Schepp's
testimony, claiming that he was as much an accomplice
as the other three men. Justice John Goff overruled the
objections. Rose supplied much of the colorful testimony
of the trial. He said he had not gone to the vicinity of

the Hotel Metropole at the time of the shooting but had
remained behind at Bridgie Webber's place.

"I was still at Webber's," he testified, "when word
came in that Rosenthal had been shot. It made me feel
sick. I laid down on the couch for a few minutes, and
then Webber suggested that I had better telephone
Becker. I asked him where we could get a booth and he
said at the Times Building. I went over there and called
him up. I said, 'Hello, there. Did you hear the news?'
'Yes,' he replied, 'I congratulate you.' 'How did you get
it so soon?' I asked. 'I got it from a newspaperman,'
he said. I said, 'Charlie, this is awful,' and he told me
not to be foolish and not to worry, that no harm would
come to anyone. He asked me where I was and I told
him at Webber's, and he said he would be down right
away."

Rose said that they waited a considerable time for
Becker before he came and they talked in the doorway
of a building. Becker explained that he had dropped into
the West Forty-seventh Street stationhouse and learned
"they ain't got a thing." He quoted Becker as saying,
"I went in the back room and had a look at him [Rosen-
thal]. It was a pleasing sight to me. If Whitman had not
been there I would have cut his tongue out and hung
it somewhere as a warning to other squealers. Now the
only thing to do is to sit tight and don't worry. Let the
boys who did the job make a getaway and lay low for a
few days until this thing blows over. Everybody thinks
it is just another gang fight or a gambler's feud." Becker
then directed Rose to pay the gunmen one thousand dollars. When Rose protested that he did not have that
kind of money, Becker borrowed it from Webber, say-

ing, "That'll make fifteen hundred I'll owe you. I'll slip it to you in a few days."

Since it was no secret that Whitman had plenty of ammunition to question Becker about his grafting activities, his lawyers kept the police lieutenant off the witness stand. A jury found Becker guilty and he was sentenced to die in the electric chair.

A short time later the actual gunmen were placed on trial, speedily convicted, and also sentenced to die.

Becker changed counsel after the trial and hired Joseph Shay to handle his appeal. Shay was a well-known and capable lawyer. The focal point of his attack of the conviction was the admission of Schepps's testimony.

While Becker's appeal was under consideration, the appeal of the four gunmen was processed and denied, and all were electrocuted. Almost sixteen months passed before the high court ruled on the Becker case. The court of appeals reversed the conviction and in discussing the Harlem conference wrote:

"The story itself is grossly improbable and it is related by four men of the vilest characters to save their own lives. I admit . . . the People have to use the witnesses available. But I emphatically deny that we are obliged to sign the defendant's death warrant simply because a jury has believed an improbable tale told by four vile criminals to shift the death penalty from themselves to another."

In a concurring opinion Judge Miller wrote: "The story of the Harlem conference is incredible on its face and the manner of its narration by the witnesses proves it to be a pure fabrication."

The court stated that Becker could not be convicted

unless the story of the Harlem conference was proved more completely than had been done in the first trial.

I now want to name the man from whom I received the confidential information about what happened after the court of appeals reversed Becker's conviction. He was Lloyd Willis, a highly respected reporter for the equally highly respected *New York Times*. Willis and I were very close friends for many years. He had left his paper to serve as Whitman's secretary.

Willis told me in the strictest confidence that after the decision from the higher court, Whitman was determined to get Shay, the successful lawyer for Becker, out of the case. Shay was to defend Becker in his second trial. The lawyer had a large negligence type of practice. There was one blot on his record. Some years earlier, when Jerome was the district attorney, one of Shay's runners made an affidavit saying that he had solicited cases for Shay. The lawyer was taken to the Tombs overnight and later was suspended from practice for one year by the Bar Association.

Whitman ordered his detectives to dig up all the information they could on Shay's activities. After receiving the reports, Willis told me that Shay was called to a secret two-hour conference with Whitman in the prosecutor's private office. No one was present but these two men. The next day Shay announced his withdrawal from the Becker case and advised his client to hire Martin Manton, who later was convicted of accepting bribes while he was a United State district court judge. Manton was a specialist in negligence cases. He knew little, if anything, about trying criminal cases and nothing about the intricacies of criminal law. Becker followed Shay's

advice and hired a man with little practical experience in
a case where a man's life was at stake. I do not believe
that the suggestion that Manton be named came solely
from Shay. He knew too many capable criminal lawyers.

I knew Shay and shortly after he had dropped out of
the case I asked him why he was not defending Becker.
If he had won, it would have established his reputation as
one of the best lawyers in New York and it would have
been worth a fortune to him in future fees. He told me
he was too busy trying a number of accident cases he had
neglected. This was before Willis told me what had happened.

The reader can elect to believe that the two-hour conference in Whitman's office with Shay was nothing more
than a social visit. Willis did not believe it and neither
do I. Whitman, in his anxiety to get Becker, overstepped
the bounds of fair play and justice—he was denying a
defendant the right to his free choice of counsel to defend him, a fundamental and basic right in our law.

With Shay out of the way, the next step was to find
a new witness to the conference that Rose, Webber,
Vallon and Schepps claimed had taken place in Harlem.
It was now over two years since the incident was supposed
to have occurred. His four talking witnesses came up with
information that James Marshall, a Negro tap dancer,
who had been a stool pigeon for Becker in getting evidence against Negro gambling places in Harlem, might
be able to verify the story.

The task of finding Marshall was assigned to a young
deputy assistant district attorney in Whitman's office.
Marshall was found and once again Becker was placed
on trial. Marshall testified that he saw Becker and Rose

together in Harlem one night about the vague time the conference was assumed to have been held. The jury believed Marshall, and Becker again was convicted. The court of appeals also accepted his testimony and the conviction this time was upheld.

However, what the jury, the court of appeals, and the public never knew was that Marshall's testimony had been obtained by direct threats from the district attorney's office that he would be prosecuted for perjury on a completely different matter. Nor was it known that for weeks before the trial, Marshall had been accompanied on his theatrical engagements by the young assistant district attorney and a detective; that he was little more than a prisoner, with the constant reminder by the presence of the two men that he could be arrested for perjury. This witness, too, was earning immunity from Whitman, so it is possible that his testimony might be prejudiced by that fact.

It was after the court of appeals upheld the conviction that Marshall let part of the cat out of the bag. He told two Philadelphia reporters that his testimony against Becker had been false. The reporters notified Becker's attorney, who obtained an affidavit from Marshall contradicting the testimony he had given at the trail. Marshall was brought back to New York and taken to the district attorney's office. After a conference there he signed a new affidavit repudiating his Philadelphia statements and stating that his original testimony had been the truth.

Whitman realized one part of his dream. On November 3, 1914, due largely to the publicity he had received in prosecuting Becker, he was elected governor of New

York. He was holding that office when the court of appeals upheld the second conviction and defense attorneys had the task of appealing for executive clemency against the death penalty to the very man who had prosecuted Becker. It occasioned no great surprise when Whitman turned down the appeal, clearing the way for the execution. There was criticism from some prominent people who said Whitman should not have sat at the clemency hearing. He replied that he did not have the authority to abdicate or delegate any duties of the governor to anyone else. Technically, he was correct, but he knew as well as anybody else that if he had taken a brief vacation out of the state at the time of the clemency hearing, the acting governor would have had the power to make any decision he thought proper and so Whitman would have avoided placing himself in an awkward position. That he did not do so may be considered an indication that he wanted to be sure that no clemency was granted to Becker.

Becker had planned to read a statement to reporters in the death chamber, but when he was informed that it would not be allowed, he issued what he termed, "My Dying Statement," in advance. It read:

Gentlemen: I stand before you in my whole senses, knowing that no power on earth can save me from the grave that is to receive me. On the face of that, in the teeth of those who condemn me and in the presence of my God and your God, I proclaim my absolute innocence of the foul crime for which I must die. You are now about to witness my destruction by the State, which is organized to protect the lives of the innocent. May Almighty God pardon everyone who has contributed in any degree to my untimely death.

And now, on the brink of the grave, I declare to the world that

I am proud to have been the husband of the purest, noblest woman that ever lived—Helen Becker. This acknowledgement is the only legacy I can leave her. I bid you all good-bye. Father, I am ready to go. Amen!

There is one further footnote to be added to this strange case. After Becker's execution, the young assistant district attorney who had obtained Marshall's testimony against Becker was appointed a magistrate on the recommendation of Whitman. About a year later he returned home from a dinner he had attended and committed suicide by shooting himself.

Whether Becker was innocent or guilty is a question each reader will have to decide for himself. I have given information not previously known and information which may very well have influenced a jury to bring in a different verdict. I never have been able to understand why, if Becker ordered the shooting, he needed so many intermediaries in plotting a murder.

While I have doubts as to the guilt of Becker for the murder, I am in no way condoning his actions as a crooked police officer. Graft and corruption exist and will continue to exist as long as some people like to gamble. There will always be those who will cater to this desire. Since the profits are large, they are willing to pay for protection and so corruption begins. Because few citizens regard gambling as a heinous crime, people are indifferent even when they know gambling is going on all around them. The result of their indifference is the weakening of the fabric of their own government and they should not be surprised at the periodic corruption scandals that break out in any city, regardless of size.

If I have learned anything in my almost one hundred years on earth, it is the futility of legislating against the desires of people where there is no clearly understood evil; if it is debatable, then it is useless. My experiences in visiting my first speak-easy back in the 1880's in Maine left no doubt in my mind what would happen when that Noble Experiment began in 1918. It was not the dregs of Eastport that I met in the back room of the candy store but the very pillars of the town, the banker, the postmaster, the leading merchants. We will have graft and corruption just as long as we have leading pillars who will assist in the breaking of laws. This does not make it right; grafters should be sought out and vigorously prosecuted, but it is a fact of life.

CHAPTER ELEVEN

Little Napoleon

FOR SOME UNEXPLAINED reason the coroner's office seemed to attract an unusual number of characters. These included the lawyers who hung around like leeches, the newspaper reporters who covered the office, and the coroners themselves. I never knew what to expect.

One of the young reporters at that time was Raymond Ditmars, who was working for the *New York Times*. He sauntered into my room one day carrying a small, battered piece of luggage that was ready to fall apart and asked if he could leave it with me. I dropped it onto the floor next to my desk, a short distance away from my feet, and he went off to make the rounds of the building. Several times that morning I was disturbed by hissing sounds and looked around but could see nothing.

Ditmars returned several hours later. Once again there was the hissing noise and I looked around again.

"Oh, my friend is angry," Ditmars said, opening the bag. Out popped the head of a huge snake! He deftly grabbed it, forced it back into the bag and closed it. Ditmars was torn between his work and his love of nature. He left the newspaper and in time became curator of reptiles of the New York Zoological Gardens and a world-famous herpetologist. Ditmars had not been thoughtless; he assured me that despite its dangerous appearance the snake was harmless. I took his word for it, but accepted no more packages from him.

There were many well-known newspapermen, including Damon Runyon, John Ward O'Malley and Ike White, who came to the office, particularly to cover inquests in the important murder cases.

Although coroners were not judges, they could sit as committing magistrates. Many of these men were from humble orgins and some of them would have had difficulty reading the simple words in comics. The wily lawyers who specialized in practicing in our court would flatter these men by constantly referring to them as "Your Honor," and with each mention of the phrase or title you could almost see the coroners swell and puff with pride.

At one point I decided to record the remarks of one of these lawyers to such a coroner who was presiding at an inquest. "Your Honor," he began, "I think, Your Honor, that we should, Your Honor . . ." The point of my pencil snapped here and I decided I had enough.

The appearance of William Howe, who had teamed up with Abe Hummel to form a notorious law firm, was always an event, particularly when he was facing a new coroner. His reputation as one of the great courtroom orators was widely known. He was a burly man who took pride in his dazzlingly expensive clothes, with a fresh rose or a carnation always pinned to his lapel, and a huge diamond stud in the bosom of his shirt. He would overwhelm the new man with his flow of multisyllabic words, his citation of legal decisions, some of which he unquestionably made up at the spur of the moment, and would pretty much run the inquest the way he wanted. Since these were mainly murder cases, his clients were held anyway, but he enjoyed his own oratory.

Most new coroners suspected a murder plot in almost every case involving an accidental death, and Antonio Zucca, with whom I entered the office, was no exception. Zucca had been born in Italy and became a very successful and wealthy importer here. He was the president of the Italian Chamber of Commerce and prominent in many of his countrymen's social organizations. While he spoke English fairly well, he did have a heavy accent.

One hot night we were notified that police had found the body of a man lying on the sidewalk in front of a tenement on Tenth Avenue near Fiftieth Street. We went to the scene and learned that the dead man, Patrick McCarthy, had boarded with Mr. and Mrs. Michael Mulligan, who lived on the top floor of the building.

The Mulligans said they had been drinking ale with McCarthy and had left him seated at the open front window of the apartment when they went to bed. We learned that Mulligan and McCarthy were good friends and that the dead man was a heavy drinker. Both were husky longshoremen. No neighbors had heard any noise from the Mulligan apartment and there were no indications that any struggle had taken place. It appeared to be a clear case of accidental death. McCarthy had probably leaned out of the window in search of a vagrant breeze, lost his balance and toppled to the street.

For no accountable reason the case looked suspicious to Zucca, and he indicated to me that he would break the Mulligans down at the inquest. Mrs. Mulligan took the stand, told her story and then Zucca questioned her.

"Now, Madam," he inquired, "you're sure you no make the goo-goo eyes at McCarthy, and he no make the goo-goo eyes at you?"

The witness straightened in her chair. She folded her massive arms across her ample bosom, glared at the coroner and in a brogue you could cut with a knife said, "Goo-goo eyes, and shure what are those?"

Zucca beat a hasty retreat. After listening to all the witnesses the coroner's jury returned with a verdict of accidental death, which I am sure it was.

But of all those I met in my years with the office it was the man we called "Little Napoleon" who was my favorite character. He was Julius Harburger, a Tammany Hall leader of an assembly district, a professional office holder, who in his long career had been a court clerk, an assemblyman, excise commissioner, and finally was elected a coroner.

Harburger was five feet five inches in height, wore a drooping silvery white mustache, which, when he was in a thoughtful frame of mind, he would pull at to the fascination of spectators, and he had mild, kindly brown eyes which he tried, in vain, to infuse with a look of harshness and authority. Because of his size he thought he bore a startling resemblance to Napoleon, and a photograph of this military genius was on prominent display in his office. He probably regretted that modern clothes prevented him from wearing the kind of costume Napoleon had worn, and whenever called to the scene of a death, he invariably would assume a Napoleonic pose, thrusting one hand into his coat bosom and holding the other clenched behind his back. Then he would walk back and forth, snapping out occasional orders and comments on the case. The only actual physical resemblance to Napoleon was his height.

Reporters doted on Harburger and he doted on them. His one great passion was to get his name in the papers, and he counted a day lost when some story using his name did not appear. He did not mind how ridiculous a story might make him appear, and when reporters learned this they really poured it on at times. A story was a story to him as long as his name was mentioned and spelled correctly. He could be ruthless and unscrupulous in maneuvering cases to get some publicity value out of them, but at the same time he was thoroughly honest; he could not be bribed, nor would he take political dictation where it would thwart justice.

He was the bane of hotel owners and managers, and they would turn livid at the sight of him. Harburger had discovered that a death in a hotel usually was good for at least a paragraph in a paper, since many guests were well-known figures, and so he left standing orders that he was to be notified immediately of any death in a hotel. Such places, quite naturally, do not like to have their names associated with death, whether it be from natural causes, suicide, or, particularly, murder.

One evening Harburger was notified that a death had occurred at the old Waldorf-Astoria, then at Thirty-fourth Street and Fifth Avenue. The hotel doctor had been called in when a guest was stricken with a heart attack and had attended him during his final hours. There was no question that death had been due to natural causes. That made no difference to Harburger. He telephoned several reporters, met them and descended on the hotel. He arrived there at the time the lobby and the hotel's famous "Peacock Alley" were crowded with people for the dinner hour.

Flanked by the reporters, Harburger marched up to the desk clerk and in a voice that could be heard clearly fifty feet away bellowed that he had come to investigate a death in the hotel.

The harried clerk whispered in an agitated voice for him to step inside the office. "No, I won't step inside," Harburger shouted. "Take me to the body at once." Excited guests by now were beginning to move toward the desk.

The little coroner was rushed to the elevator with his retinue. The manager, who had appeared by now, glanced at the reporters. He knew very well who they were, but he asked.

"They're my secretaries," Harburger retorted, and the hotel man had to let them enter the elevator. Once up in the hotel suite, he forced the grieving widow and the hotel doctor to be sworn and answer questions. The questions were designed to fill in the reporters on the information they wanted. Satisfied at last, he said the coroner's physician would appear later to issue a death certificate, and departed. Actually, all that had been necessary in the case, since a reputable doctor was involved, was to have the coroner's physician go there and issue the certificate. If the physician had not been satisfied, he then could have notified the coroner that an investigation was necessary. But the grateful reporters used the story, and Harburger's name appeared in the papers.

One of his most notable exploits was his one-man assault upon the Imperial German Navy of Kaiser Wilhelm II.

His Majesty's cruiser, *Hertha,* had anchored in the North River for an official visit to New York. While transferring coal aboard the vessel, one of the sailors was killed when a sack fell on him. A foreign warship is beyond the jurisdiction of the New York police, the coroner, or even the United States government. It was German territory and the exclusive business of the Imperial Navy. The only way we even knew of the death was through a request from the commander of the vessel asking permission to have the man buried ashore with naval honors.

As soon as he heard about it, Coroner Harburger dashed to a police launch and directed a patrolman to take him to the *Hertha's* landing ladder.

When the launch approached the side of the warship, an officer called down and inquired what was wanted. Harburger shouted back that he was the coroner and wanted to come aboard to investigate the death of the sailor. The startled officer coldly informed Harburger that he had no business aboard the vessel.

"Oh, but I'm the coroner, you know," the irrepressible little man shouted back. "Look. Here's my shield." He then stated that he would refuse to allow the body to be taken ashore until he had made an investigation. The baffled officer, not knowing that Harburger possessed no such power, consulted with the ship's commander, and Harburger was invited aboard. He was taken to the chief

medical officer, who assured him the sailor's death had
been an accident. The medical officer bowed, Harburger
bowed, and he left.

Upon returning to our office, his first action was to call
in newsmen and he related word-for-word his adventure.
He also said, "I think that this is the first time in the
history of the coroner's office that a coroner has gone
aboard a foreign man-of-war to investigate a case. They
tried to stop me from going aboard, but I let them understand that Coroner Julius Harburger was not to be in-
timidated in the performance of his duties."

The press gave Harburger full treatment and each
story was funnier than the next. A thin-skinned man
would have left town for several days, but Harburger
enjoyed every word written and was willing to show you
the clippings at a moment's notice.

What pleased Harburger the most was to be connected
with a mystery, since this meant that it would be a continuing story in the paper and he would be quoted in
addition to having his name printed. Such mysteries do
not happen often, and Harburger would do his best to
create one.

On the morning of October 1, 1906, Al Adams, the
notorious policy king, who had recently been released
from jail, was found dead in his room at the Ansonia
Hotel. There was a bullet hole in his temple, and a .44-
caliber Colt revolver was lying on the floor by his chair.
Coroner Harburger was on duty when the call came in.

His first act, as usual, was to notify the newspapers and
he asked that reporters be sent to meet him at the Ansonia.
Detectives, who already had made their investigation,
knew that it was a case of suicide.

Harburger went to the room, viewed the body, examined the gun, and then questioned every single employee in the hotel from the manager to the last bellhop. The weary detectives suggested at the end that Harburger close it out as a suicide so that they could get back to their other work. The little coroner would hear no such talk. He knew that if he called it a suicide, the case would be over in the newspapers and his publicity short-lived. But if he kept the case open and hinted at murder, there would be high excitement in the press, at least until after the inquest, and the inquest itself would be fully reported.

When he went down to the lobby he met the reporters who already had received the essential facts from the detectives. They simply were waiting for the official verdict. "It is a suicide?" one of them asked.

Harburger drew himself up into his Napoleonic pose and replied with an extremely serious expression on his face, "Boys, it looks very suspicious. I must investigate the case further. It may be a murder."

That was enough for the reporters. They broke for the telephones and soon the presses were rolling with headlines quoting Harburger that the Adams death might be a murder.

This went on for several days, until the inquest. There had been no further investigation by our office because there was nothing to investigate.

The owner of the hotel was Stokes, a financier. He was frantic at the unfavorable publicity, since the daily stories always mentioned his hotel. He had talked to police and to District Attorney Jerome and knew they were convinced that Adams had shot himself.

Shortly before the inquest began, Stokes walked into Harburger's office, refused to shake hands with him, and berated him for what he was doing to his hotel. He said there had been ten thousand dollars' worth of room cancellations.

Harburger was not to be slighted in his own office. "I want you to know that this is the most important office of the people," he yelled.

The two men then began trading shouted insults and at one point when Stokes, who was perspiring freely, reached for a handkerchief, Harburger bellowed, "Are you going to pull the gun that you used on Al Adams?" He knew reporters were congregated outside his door.

When the inquest opened, Harburger described the circumstances of Adams' death and said to the jury, "It is for you gentlemen to decide, after hearing the testimony of the witnesses, whether this is a suicide or a murder." He then stared at Stokes and added, "If you find that it is a murder, the murderer may be sitting in this room."

Stokes started to his feet and had to be pulled back by his lawyer.

The testimony was short and to the point. There was absolutely no evidence of any kind to indicate that the case was anything but a suicide. Although Harburger tried to stretch out the proceedings by having the jury retire to consider a verdict, the foreman announced that it would not be necessary; the jury already had reached the conclusion that Adams had shot himself.

Despite his ardent belief in the value of publicity of any kind, Harburger, to his bitter disappointment, was defeated when he ran for re-election.

With his political connections, he could not be kept down. Tammany Hall had him appointed a deputy state comptroller and later rewarded him with a term of sheriff, one of the most lucrative posts in the city. The sheriff's office was largely a civil one concerned with the service of papers for which the sheriff collected a fee. Many men became wealthy from the legal fees they collected in that office.

Harburger was not particularly happy there, despite the money, because there was little chance for publicity. He had greatly cherished his office as coroner because of the opportunities it gave him for getting his name in the papers. As a matter of fact, few offices in the city, with the exception of the mayor and the district attorney, were so much in the public eye.

He sent for reporters on one occasion while sheriff to expound on the theory that the electric chair might only stun the victim and that the real execution occurred when the doctor performed an autopsy after the electrocution. He remarked that his interest was aroused because of cases of temporary suspended animation that he had observed as coroner. When reporters questioned me, I had to tell them that we never had heard of a case of suspended animation in the coroner's office. His suggestion that he be allowed to attend an electrocution and attempt to revive the man was rejected by the prison warden.

When he died in 1914, the *New York Sun* referred to him as unique in the political and municipal activities of which he was a part. He was not created after any model, and everybody who met him will say there never will be another man like Julius Harburger.

I have no doubt that had Harburger been alive to

read the tribute, he would have agreed without reservation to everything that was said about him. There is no question that he enriched joyously the archives of the city.

CHAPTER TWELVE

The Fresh Breeze

THE CORRUPTION SCANDALS caused by the greed of some coroners, the undisputed fact that politicians could and did fix cases before coroner's juries, and the appalling incompetence of some of the coroners and coroner's physicians led to a demand by doctors, lawyers and others for the abolition of the office and its replacement by the medical examiner system.

When John P. Mitchell, a reform mayor, took office in 1914, he asked Commissioner of Accounts Leonard M. Wallstein to investigate the coroner's office. Even though Wallstein missed most of the real scandals of the office, and Mayor Mitchell even had to apologize for some of the unfounded rumors the commissioner accepted as true without any investigation, the few actual facts that Wallstein did bring out shocked the public.

Wallstein's report, issued the following year, pointed

out what we already knew; that some of the coroners were virtually illiterate, that many were political hacks who had been plumbers, milkmen, saloonkeepers. One was even a tombstone cutter. There was nothing wrong or dishonorable with their previous occupations, but their working experiences hardly qualified them for the important position they held. Only some of the coroners had been doctors.

Most of the coroner's physicians were not qualified to do autopsy work and the few who were became the work horses of the office. All the important cases were assigned to them, whether they were on duty or not, and they remained in office as coroners came and went to make certain that we could function. I believe that some of the coroner's physicians were graduates of diploma mills rather than reputable medical schools. There were a few whose medical ability I so doubted that I would not have trusted them to prescribe an aspirin for a common cold. These men were political appointees selected for their ability to swing votes and not a scalpel.

Wallstein's report left little doubt as to what he thought of these doctors when he wrote:

Numerous homicides have undoubtedly failed of detection by reason of the incompetent work of the coroner's physicians. The character of their medical examination may be judged from the fact that the keeper of the morgue testified that they often merely looked at the head of the body and that an examination lasting five minutes was an infrequent occasion. Some of the coroner's physicians have favorite causes of death which, without shadow of reason, they are in the habit of assigning in cases of doubt.

The legislature in 1915 passed a law abolishing the coroner's office and ordered it to be replaced by the medical examiner system. A delay was granted, though, with the new office to go into effect on January 1, 1918.

Let me say at this point that both parties, the Democrats and the Republicans, were equally guilty in bringing the coroner's office into disrepute. As I mentioned earlier, two of the worst crooks in the office were elected to replace Tammany men. Yet the coroner's office could and did do important work.

Like almost all reform mayors, Mitchell lasted just one term, losing his bid for re-election, and John F. Hylan, "Red Mike," as he became known because of his flaming hair, took office on January 1, 1918. It was the duty of the new mayor to appoint the new chief medical examiner and start the office going. The appointment was to be made from a list of men who had passed a special examination qualifying them for lifetime appointment. One of the purposes of the new office was to remove it from the influence of politics which a lifetime appointment guaranteed.

The new mayor appointed Dr. Patrick Reardon, a former coroner, as chief medical examiner, and explained that Dr. Reardon's appointment was strictly a temporary one, which could be made legally for thirty days, in order to give him time to study the qualifications of the various candidates.

Dr. Charles Norris was appointed on February 18, 1918. Although technically he was the second man to hold the office, he always has been considered the first chief medical examiner of New York City because he was the first qualified man, and a fresh breeze blew through what was once the coroner's office. Dr. Norris was not a political appointee; in fact, his only flaw was an almost pathological dislike of politicians; to him, they were all bad. His appointment had been demanded by the people because he was so eminently qualified. He was recognized as one of this country's outstanding pathologists, had taught the subject at the Columbia University medical school, and had been director for many years of the Bellevue Hospital laboratories.

He brought with him a tremendous enthusiasm and a brilliant and inquiring mind that was never satisfied with anything but perfection. Startled young doctors, who already were making a name for themselves in pathology and allied fields, found themselves dragooned into serving as his assistants at salaries far below what they could have earned elsewhere, and they stayed.

Well over six feet tall and weighing some two hundred pounds, Dr. Norris even in middle age looked like a plunging football back, and he had been a member of one of Yale's great football teams. When I first met him his hair was graying, as were his mustache and his trim Van Dyke. He had shaggy eyebrows which were whiter than his hair, and the contrast made his dark eyes appear even more stern and piercing than they were.

In reality, he was a very kind man. He hadn't been in office very long when he realized that while some of the medical assistants he had to retain were competent, they were not of the top-drawer quality he was demanding. He did not want to embarrass these men or injure their reputations, and he asked me what could be done. I quietly arranged to have them transferred to other city departments where their qualifications were more suitable, and they were happy to escape from the office.

Although I had always been considered the secretary

to the board of coroners, there was no such authorized position. But the new medical examiner's office did provide for an official secretary, and Dr. Norris appointed me to this post. I was to work closely with him during the sixteen years that I remained with the office.

He assembled his staff with great care and appointed Dr. Alexander O. Gettler as his toxicologist. These two men, Dr. Norris and Dr. Gettler, were indefatigable. Long after everybody else had gone home they were at work in the laboratory, blazing new trails that made medico-legal history and transformed a run-down office into the outstanding one in the world.

There was one important difference between the medical examiner system and the former coroner procedure. Immediately upon notification of a homicide or a suspicious death, it was the Chief or one of his assistants who went at once to the scene. No one was allowed to touch the body until one of them arrived. All of these men were skilled pathologists and experts in microscopy. The undisturbed scene often could tell them as much as an autopsy.

When Dr. Norris entered the office he discovered that there was very little reliable information available on gunshot wounds. He promptly collected a sample of every type of weapon known and then he and a detective spent weeks discharging the guns into all kinds of available material, from every possible angle, and at varying ranges. When he finished he had compiled data on powder burns and shot patterns that still is a standard in use all over the world.

A new breed of detective was making its way into the force. Men who looked upon their work as a career, eager and anxious to learn, they flocked to the morgue to watch autopsies and receive pointers from Dr. Norris. He was "Chief" to everybody and it got so that he rarely heard his own name mentioned.

He was particularly interested in performing the autopsies in homicide cases and there always was a circle of men around him as he worked and explained his findings.

On one of these typical days at the morgue, the Chief would perform several post-mortems and then ask the detectives to join him. He had fixed up a small cluttered office next to the morgue proper that was called the Country Club. He would bring out a bottle of rye from a closet—one was always there, even during prohibition— and then he would discuss the fine points of detecting murder. If anybody praised him for his incredible skill in ferreting out signs of homicide, his favorite retort was, "Go easy on that detective stuff, old man. You can't make an old son of a sea cook like me into a detective. You can't make a fat-bellied doctor into a sleuth." Secretly, he was pleased.

When Vincent Coll, the gangster known as the Mad Dog, was machine-gunned by his enemies while in a telephone booth on West Twenty-third Street, Dr. Norris took a scientific interest in the wounds.

He promptly issued a warning to police that the open emergency wagons they were using in responding to riot calls were useless against such a weapon. "One man with a machine gun could stand in a second-story window and wipe out an entire wagon of police," he said. "The men wouldn't have a fighting chance."

Coll's body had at least eighteen bullet holes, and

Dr. Norris said that each machine-gun bullet had left a hole as big as the bottom of a teacup, as if the flesh had been hacked out with a hatchet. Police switched to closed emergency wagons.

Dr. Norris was doubted by police just once, when he first came into office. A patrolman walking his beat in the early morning hours on the Brooklyn waterfront, passed a man carrying a heavy bundle over his shoulders. More bored than suspicious, he asked the man what he was carrying.

"Just my working clothes," the other replied. "I'm on my way to work at the next pier."

The officer told him to go ahead and resumed his walk, twirling his club. As he reached the next corner he glanced back and saw that the man had deposited his bundle on the stringpiece of a dock and was watching him. His suspicions now aroused, the alert officer started to go back. When the man on the dock noticed this, he hurriedly kicked the bundle into the water and started running. The officer set out in pursuit and grabbed the man, who still insisted it was just his old clothes he had thrown away.

The prisoner was taken to the local precinct where he was identified as Francisco Trapia, a longshoreman living on Sackett Street in Brooklyn. Officers were sent to the pier and started dragging for the bundle thrown into the water, while others went to the Sackett Street tenement and broke open the door of Trapia's flat. Propped up against the kitchen wall was the headless torso of a woman. Near it lay her severed head. The arms and legs were missing.

Trapia was rushed back, under police escort, to his

flat and as soon as he entered the kitchen he broke down and confessed. He admitted cutting up the torso. He said that he and the woman had been drinking heavily and when he awakened he found her dead. He reasoned that he must have killed her during the night and he cut up the body hoping to dispose of it.

Our office was notified as a matter of routine, and Dr. Norris hurried to the tenement with one of his Brooklyn assistants. The Chief examined the head and torso of the woman, noticed the familiar cherry-red mottling that indicated monoxide poisoning, and told the open-mouthed detectives that it did not look like murder at all, but like death from asphyxiation caused by a faulty stove flue. The remains were taken to the morgue for an autopsy.

With a confession from the longshoreman on their hands, police went ahead with their arrest, and the district attorney agreed with them, obtaining an indictment for first-degree murder. During the trial the officer testified how he had observed the suspicious actions of Trapia, other officers told of finding the severed remains, and Trapia's confession was read. There was little doubt that a jury at that point would have convicted the long-shoreman. The defense called Dr. Norris to the stand, and his autopsy report made it plain that the woman had died in her sleep from the odorless but deadly fumes escaping from the stove. The husky longshoreman habitually arose early, and this probably saved his life. He was groggy, thought it was due to a hang-over and opened the windows. When he discovered the woman was dead, he panicked and thought he had killed her. The man was promptly acquitted by a jury. Dr. Norris established that the medical examiner's office was not interested in obtaining convictions but was interested in the truth.

On another occasion, it was this scrupulous fidelity to truth that turned a seemingly natural death into murder.

A group of men of Greek descent were playing cards when Constantinos Zalianos was stabbed by George Valsopolous. The latter disappeared while Zalianos was taken to the hospital, where to the surprise of doctors he recovered. The injured man had no interest in pressing charges, and police discontinued their search. Several years passed, Zalianos became ill and died. Everybody assumed that it was due to natural causes, but Dr. Norris recalled the severe stab wounds and ordered an autopsy. The medical findings showed that the long-delayed death still was due to the effects of the knife wounds. Police traced Valsopolous to New Jersey. He was arrested and convicted.

Dr. Norris always referred to the murder of Joseph B. Elwell, the bridge expert, as "the classic mystery." Few people know that this celebrated case was almost closed out by police and the district attorney as a suicide, and it was only upon Dr. Norris' insistence that they finally realized they had a puzzling murder on their hands, one which is still listed as unsolved.

It was about eight-ten on the morning of June 11, 1920, when Mrs. Marie Larsen, Elwell's housekeeper, arrived at his private house on West Seventieth Street. She entered the vestibule, picked up a bottle of milk, and then let herself in with her key.

As she walked by the living room she noticed some

letters on the floor and glanced into the room. The
bridge expert, clad in pajamas and barefooted, was
slumped in a chair, a bullet hole in the exact center
of his forehead. He was alive and breathing noisily. The
housekeeper at first failed to recognize him because he
was not wearing his toupee and his false teeth. He was
never seen without either.

The frightened woman ran shrieking out into the
street, stopped a milkman and asked him to get help,
but meanwhile kept running up the block until she
found a patrolman. The officer returned with her and
asked the milkman to help him.

"When I entered," the milkman said later, "I saw the
wounded man sitting in a chair. His head was hanging
over the chair, his right arm hanging limp, with the
fingers sort of crooked. There was a pool of blood on
the floor just back of the chair, and blood was flowing
from a wound in his forehead. It looked to me as if he'd
been shot just a few minutes before I saw him. I thought
it was suicide."

And so did Captain Arthur Carey, veteran head of the
homicide squad, and District Attorney Edward Swann.
Elwell had been internationally known, and the shooting
of such a man had sent both of them racing to the house.
Elwell already had been taken by ambulance to the
hospital, but everything else had been left untouched.
Although Elwell still was alive, Dr. Norris also was
notified and he went to the scene.

There was much in the early information police
gathered to support a suicide theory. Elwell had received
his morning mail. Detectives established that the post-
man had delivered the letters at seven-thirty-five, ringing

the bell twice. Elwell probably had come downstairs
from his bedroom to get the letters. He was a vain person,
and the fact that he was not wearing his toupee and his
dentures indicated that he was not expecting visitors.
The mailman had gone up and down the stoops on the
street for ten minutes, the house had been in his sight
all that time, and he had not seen anyone near the Elwell
home.

Nothing was disturbed inside. There were no indications of any struggle. Elwell had been seated in a chair
in the living room. Just one shot, a .45, had been fired,
and the bullet had gone through his skull, hit the wall
behind him, where it gouged out some plaster, and then
richocheted to the top of a lamp table beside him. His
wallet, containing four hundred dollars in cash, was upstairs in his room near his hairpiece and dentures. Mrs.
Larsen arrived at eight-ten and saw nobody. A milkman
working on the block also said the street had been deserted. Elwell still was bleeding profusely, indicating
the shooting had occurred not too long before Mrs. Larsen arrived. There was no gun around, but police already
had learned that Mrs. Larsen had hidden a woman's
pink nightgown to avoid embroiling her employer in any
scandal and so they reasoned that she also had hidden
the gun, despite her denials. It is not at all uncommon
for friends or members of a family to hide a weapon
in an attempt to disguise a suicide.

After observing the scene, Dr. Norris went to the
hospital, where he was informed that Elwell was dying.
He left instructions to be notified as soon as death occurred because he wanted to perform an immediate
autopsy.

Meanwhile, District Attorney Swann ordered Dr. Otto Schultze, his medical assistant, to investigate. The latter arrived at Bellevue just after Elwell died and before Dr. Norris could reach the morgue.

Dr. Schultze examined the body and stated that the wound had been self-inflicted. He was a well-known pathologist and had served as a coroner's psysician, during the course of which service he had performed some six thousand autopsies. In addition, he also held the chair of medical jurisprudence at a medical school. He based his suicide verdict on the powder marks on Elwell's forehead which showed the gun had been fired at close range.

When Dr. Norris arrived, he performed an autopsy and flatly contradicted Dr. Schultze. He insisted Elwell had been murdered and told Carey and Swann:

"Elwell was drilled through the head, right in the center of his eyebrows. There was about three inches of powder burns around the wound indicating that the revolver had been held at least four or five inches away. He could never have inflicted that wound himself. No man can hold a forty-five calibre that far away and shoot himself straight through the head."

Those weeks Dr. Norris had spent in firing the different weapons and measuring the powder burns now proved their value. Carey and Swann finally agreed that they had a murder on their hands, although it took a thorough search of the house and neighborhood before the prosecutor would admit it. "Only for the disappearance of the gun I would be convinced that Elwell was a suicide," he commented.

Mrs. Larsen said that Elwell also employed a secretary

and a chauffeur but lived alone in the large home, the employees leaving by 6:00 P.M. He usually dined out.

A search of the house soon disclosed why Elwell preferred to have no help about after dark. In an adjoining bedroom, detectives found an expensive pink nightgown and a matching pair of slippers. Mrs. Larsen said she did not know the name of the woman who wore the garments and she indicated there had been a steady parade of women in Elwell's life.

This was verified by a search of his desk. A card index contained the names, initials, nicknames, addresses and telephone numbers of fifty-three different women. There also were hundreds of photographs of women from different strata of society, some, members of society, others, chorus girls. Concealed under several pads of paper was a list of women with notations alongside each showing that Elwell had been sending them checks every month. Canceled checks and voucher stubs indicated that he had pensioned off many of his ex-mistresses.

Telephone records showed that Elwell had received an incoming call at 3:00 A.M. and at 4:30 A.M. had placed the first of two calls to Far Rockaway, neither of which was answered.

Elwell had opened just one of the letters he had received. It was from his horse trainer in Covington and reported on the condition of several horses he owned.

About noon a woman telephoned and asked for Elwell. A quick-thinking detective told her to come right over, that Elwell was sick. A short time later an attractive brunette hurried up the front steps, ran a gauntlet of reporters and entered the house. Authorities refused to reveal her identity to newspaper reporters, although they admitted she was the woman who wore the pink night-gown. Reporters dubbed her "The Lady in Pink."

She was Viola Kraus, member of a socially prominent family. Her sister was married to Walter Lewisohn. She was able to account for the murdered man's time the previous evening. She and Elwell had dined at the Ritz-Carlton with her sister and brother-in-law. It was in the nature of a celebration party; she had just received her final divorce decree that day from Victor von Schlegell, a former Yale football star and a wealthy executive. As they were being seated, a couple was ushered to an adjoining table. It was von Schlegell and an attractive blonde.

She said there had been an awkward pause for a few moments, but Elwell and von Schlegell, who had known each other for years, nodded cordially and the two groups ignored each other after that. Following dinner they went to the New Amsterdam Theater roof where they were joined by Octavio Figueroa, a well-known South American journalist. While they were telling him of their experiences at the Ritz-Carlton, von Schlegell and his blond companion stepped off the elevator for the second encounter of the night.

Miss Kraus added that her ex-husband left after the performance but their group remained until 2:00 A.M. She and Elwell quarreled just before their party broke up. When they emerged on the street, all except Elwell piled into one taxi. They lived on the East Side, while his home was on the West Side.

A taxidriver was found who had picked up Elwell near the theater shortly after 2:00 A.M. He had been alone and asked to be taken to his home. He had stopped once to buy a racing paper. The cabbie said he had remained parked in front of the house to make out his route sheet and saw Elwell enter the house alone, using his key. His route sheet showed the time of arrival at two-thirty.

Miss Kraus said she had made the incoming call at 3:00 A.M. She had telephoned to patch up their spat and had made a golfing date for later that day. Her call at noon had been made to verify the arrangements.

Von Schlegell was able to present an airtight alibi of his movements. He said the two meetings on the previous night had been a coincidence that is bound to happen in New York where certain hotels and cafés are considered the smart place to go. His companion was a voice student, who had been leaving that night for Minneapolis, and he had allowed her to select the places to which she wanted to go. The young woman was contacted in her home town, returned to New York and confirmed von Schlegell's statements. The couple later were married.

The two calls Elwell had made to Far Rockaway were to the number of W. H. Pendleton, Elwell's partner in a racing stable. Pendleton said he had been home and had not received any calls during the night. An extension telephone was in a maid's room where she took calls when her employer was out. She also stated the telephone had not rung during the night. Pendleton added that Elwell had never called him at that early hour in the three years of their association.

At one time Elwell had passed out keys to his home to the various women in his life, but just two weeks before he was shot, he realized that this could lead to an embarrassing situation if two of them came at the same time, and so he had changed his lock. Only two keys

were made for the new lock, one for himself and the
other for his housekeeper.

About the only thing police learned from their inquiry
into the fifty-three women listed on the index cards was
that Elwell had been most discreet in his affairs of the
heart and had managed to carry them on without any
scandal. He had been separated from his wife for several
years and gave her two hundred dollars a month plus support for their son. One of the unopened letters had been
from his son, who was away at school. His wife had been
satisfied with the financial arrangements and knew that
she was not mentioned in his will, so she could gain
nothing by his death.

It was equally puzzling as to how the killer had entered and left. A painter was at work next door when
the mailman deposited the letters for Elwell. He saw
the housekeeper arrive and witnessed her dash outside a
minute later shouting for help. He had not seen anybody
enter or leave the house from the time the mailman called
until Mrs. Larsen arrived, nor had he heard any shot.
Neighbors, some of whom were on the street on their way
to work during the fateful hour, also said they had noticed
no strangers nor had they heard any shot.

The search for the missing .45 was thorough. Three
tons of coal in the basement were moved piece by piece.
Chimneys were scrutinized, floors and ceilings tapped for
hidden compartments, and all sewers in the area searched.
Several dozen patrolmen ruined their dispositions and
appetites as they raked through all garbage collected in
Manhattan that day. The missing weapon was never
found.

Police have expressed doubt that Elwell's killer was

a woman because a .45 automatic is not the kind of weapon a woman would use, and also because it is unlikely that the vain Elwell would have admitted a woman without his wig and false teeth. I'm not so certain. If the gun was the only weapon a woman had ready access to, she would have taken it regardless of its caliber. The fact that Elwell made no struggle, no attempt to escape, could indicate that he thought the holder of the gun was bluffing. He would be more likely to think that of a woman than of a man. It is not unlikely that some of the women in his life discovered the secret of his hair and teeth during their love-making. One thing is certain. Whoever murdered the playboy bridge expert has kept his or her mouth shut tight during the passing years.

Dr. Norris clashed with Dr. Schultze on one other case, this time Dr. Norris contending that it was a suicide and the other that it was a murder. Arthur Train, who created the famous "Mr. Tutt" stories, was the defense counsel in this case.

The body of a young woman was found on the sidewalk in front of a building on Amsterdam Avenue. While a patrolman was examining it, a man thrust his head out of the window, five stories above, and called out asking if anything was wrong. Told there was a dead woman on the street, Michael Troy came rushing down in his pajamas and identified the woman as his wife, Bessie, twenty-two.

Mike and Bessie had been married the previous May. It was now December. He was a caddy at Van Cortland Park, while his bride was employed as a page at a hotel where her father was house electrician.

Troy said that he had gone to bed before his wife came

home from work. He woke up at two-thirty, got a drink of water and noticed that Bessie had come home but apparently had gone out again. It was at this point that he heard the commotion on the street and called out.

Assistant Medical Examiner George Hohmann made the autopsy, and Dr. Norris agreed with his findings that the girl had killed herself. The body was taken to her parents' home in New Jersey and burial was held there. Her father was unwilling to believe that a bride of a few months could have taken her own life and he protested against the failure of authorities to make a proper inquiry. Dr. Schultze obtained permission to perform an autopsy. He reported finding "contusions on the throat" which he said were signs that the girl had been strangled. He was certain she had been murdered. Some blood had been found on the pillow in Troy's bedroom. He was indicted for first-degree murder.

The young man's father had been a gardener on the estate of William Earl Dodge and he appealed to Dodge for help in defending his son. Arthur Train had been a successful lawyer in New York before he began his writing career, and he was hired to defend Mike Troy.

The defense wanted Dr. Norris to make a second autopsy, but he felt it would be far better to have a complete outside opinion, and Dr. George B. Magrath, the noted Boston medical examiner, was brought in. The body of the girl was exhumed.

Puffing on his inevitable cigar, Dr. Norris later told me about it. "George," he said, "Dr. Magrath did a beautiful piece of work. Wonderful. There was a beautiful blood aspiration in the lungs that proved the woman

was alive and breathing when she hit the sidewalk."
She had not been strangled.

With the testimony of Drs. Norris, Magrath and Hohmann, Troy was acquitted. Why did Bessie Troy, young
and newly married, take her own life? That mystery was
buried with her. An autopsy can tell how a person died
but it cannot probe the mind.

Dr. Norris had one blind spot. His dislike of politicians
and of what they had done with the coroner's jury so
prejudiced him that even though the law specifically gave
the medical examiner the right to hold inquests, he refused to do so. While there may be less need for an inquest in murder cases as long as we have an efficient
police department and a district attorney, there is a
serious need for inquests in accident cases of various
kinds. Without such inquiries the public is not only de-
fenseless against practices that should be remedied but
often remains unaware of the true causes. It was an inquest held by the coroner's office, for example, that
brought out the causes for the high death toll in the
Triangle Shirtwaist factory. The jury recommended the
establishment of a fire-prevention bureau within the fire
department. This was done and has saved countless lives.
Inquests can serve a very useful function for public
welfare. After some years Dr. Norris did come around
to my view, but he pointed out that the limited budget
and the heavy case load made it impractical for him to
start holding inquests and he recommended in a report
that the city appoint a magistrate to hold such hearings.
Nothing was done, and I still feel that it is a function of
the medical examiner's office to do so. At the time of my

twenty-fifth anniversary with the office I spoke out publicly against this failure.

Dr. Norris was impatient with such matters as budgets,
and during his early years in office hostile politicians deliberately shortchanged the medical examiner. Twice
during this period he tried to resign. The first time Mayor
Hylan got him to take it back. On the other occasion I
stole his letter of resignation until I could get his assistants to talk him out of it.

He was independently wealthy and he paid for equipment out of his own pocket. He also used his own funds
to pay for a stenographer who took dictation of findings
as a post-mortem was being made.

Dr. Norris showed his contempt for politicians when
they suddenly created the office of chief assistant and
wanted him to appoint a certain member of the staff, who
was a holdover from the coroner system, to that post.
Dr. Norris accepted the new office with great joy. He felt
he now could reward a man who deserved it and he gave
the position to Dr. Thomas A. Gonzales, one of the
talented men he had persuaded to work with him. He
ignored the man the politicians wanted appointed. He
had made a wise selection. It was Dr. Gonzales who succeeded to the office after Dr. Norris died.

I was pleased when in the same year that I reached
retirement age and had to leave the office, the brilliant
work of Dr. Norris was formally recognized. On December 6, 1934, five hundred doctors gathered in the audi-
torium of the New York Academy of Medicine to watch
as he received a gold medal for distinguished service in
medicine. The citation accompanying the award read:

"He has carried on in spite of political handicaps and

has been a great factor in cleaning up the very undesirable conditions which in former times existed in the coroner's office."

Dr. Norris continued in office until his unexpected death, after one day's illness, on September 11, 1935. The world-wide reputation of the New York medical examiner's office is his monument.

CHAPTER THIRTEEN

The Singed Butterfly

A MYSTERIOUS TELE-phone call from a private detective thrust me into the opening phases of the murder of a typical Broadway butterfly and the frantic efforts of a multimillionaire social figure to cover up his own role in one of New York's most sensational cases of this century. I think this murder might have been solved if Dr. Charles Norris, the chief medical examiner, had listened to my pleas and conducted an inquiry.

There was nothing unusual about the report our office received from police headquarters shortly before noon on March 15, 1923. A Dot King, according to the information given us, had been found dead in her apartment at 144 West Fifty-seventh Street. "Nothing suspicious, no doctor," was the notation written on the slip by the clerk receiving the report from police.

When a person dies in New York City without a doctor

in attendance, the law requires the death certificate to be issued by the medical examiner, and so the Chief or an assistant always goes to the scene. With more than five thousand deaths that must be checked each year, there is a heavy case load each day, and such routine notifications are among the last to be visited. Murders, suspected homicides and accidents are given preference since these require immediate police action and the bodies cannot be moved until an examination is made at the scene by our office. The chief usually goes out only on important murder cases.

As part of my duties as secretary, I handled the assignment of cases. Dr. Cassassa, an assistant medical examiner, telephoned during the afternoon, and I added the King case to his list. He mentioned that he would hold it until last.

Shortly after three o'clock I received a telephone call from a private detective I knew, and he asked whether we had a report of a death on West Fifty-seventh Street. I glanced through the list, saw the Dot King name and mentioned it. "What about it?" I asked. "Oh, nothing, George," he replied in an offhand manner. "I'll be seeing you around one of these days."

My suspicions were immediately aroused. I knew this man normally handled work for important lawyers and banks, and from the police report there should have been nothing about this death to arouse any interest on their part. His failure to explain why he had made the call indicated that something was brewing. I was unable to locate Dr. Cassassa but left word at the places he still had to visit to go at once to the Dot King apartment. Dr. Norris was at the morgue and I did not want to take him away from his work and send him out on a possible wild-goose chase, but still worried, I went to the King apartment by taxicab.

An elevator operator took me to the fifth floor and pointed to the rear apartment. The building was actually two adjacent former private homes that had been converted into apartments. A Negro maid admitted me. I noticed two crumpled coats on the floor of the small foyer. A uniformed patrolman was seated in a chair in the living room talking to a middle-aged woman and a younger man. The officer told me they were the mother and a brother of the dead woman. The bedroom was right off the living room and the door was open. The police officer had stationed himself where he could see the body since it was his duty to guard it until after an examination by the medical examiner. I went to the doorway of the bedroom and stood stock still with shock.

The body of a blond woman in her late twenties was in a contorted position on the bed. Her head was partly buried under a pillow and you could see a large wad of cotton jammed under her nostrils. An empty bottle with chloroform on the label lay between her legs. Her left arm was twisted behind her back in a hammerlock hold. The fingers were curved like claws. I wheeled to tell the comfortably seated officer that it was a case of murder. Just then Dr. Cassassa, who had received my message, hurried in. He took one glance at the body and said, "Let's call the Chief."

It was small satisfaction to see the patrolman suddenly go into action when he learned he had been sitting placidly for hours amid such obvious signs of murder. Much valuable time had been lost for the police investigation, and *rigor mortis* already had set in, which made the actual time of death more difficult to estimate.

While waiting for Dr. Norris and the police, I questioned those in the apartment. Close to the left leg of the victim was a vest pocket comb in a leather case, the type men carry. I asked the mother and the maid whether the comb belonged to the victim, and both said it did not. The worn edges of the leather container indicated that it was habitually carried in a pocket, the obvious inference being a man's pocket, since women carry their combs in their purses. It could have dropped from the murderer's pocket during his struggles with the woman, since the condition of the bed sheets and her clawed fingers showed that she had put up a fight for her life.

Later both the mother and the maid changed their stories, one of the many changes made in this strange case.

I also questioned John Thomas, the Negro elevator operator. He told me that at seven-thirty the previous evening he had taken two men to the apartment and that an hour later they had come down with Miss King and left the building. He knew the men as Mr. Marshall and Mr. Wilson, having heard Miss King call them that. All three returned about midnight, and the elevator man said they appeared to be "pretty jolly." About half an hour later Mr. Wilson came down alone.

I asked him when Mr. Marshall left, and he said he still had not seen him when he went off duty at seven o'clock that morning.

"Could he have come down without your having seen him?" I asked. Thomas said that this could have been possible. He explained that the two buildings had been joined at the second floor by breaking halls through the

walls. Anybody could walk down to the second floor, cross
over to number 146 and exit through a door there. This
door was so arranged that it was an exit only. The only
entrance to the building was at number 144 at the
elevator.

The maid, Ella Bradford, who was called Billy, told
me that Dot King referred to Mr. Marshall as "the
millionaire." She indicated that it was not his real name
but claimed she did not know what it really was. She
thought he lived in Boston. The name of the second man,
Mr. Wilson, also seemed to be an alias. He was supposed
to be Mr. Marshall's secretary.

Mrs. Catherine Keenan, the mother of Dot King, described Mr. Marshall to me as a "fine gentleman" and
said he had been "very kind" to her daughter. She added
that he had given Dot many expensive presents of jewelry
and furs. These had disappeared from the apartment.

When I asked the maid about this, she said that before
I had arrived at the apartment, Mrs. Keenan had made
a trip to her own home, taking with her some of her
daughter's possessions. She then returned to the apartment. Why the policeman on duty permitted this I do
not know to this day.

The maid added that Mr. Marshall had been a frequent visitor and just a few days earlier had brought Dot
King "a beautiful present" upon his return from a trip
to the South. It was obvious that Dot King was being
kept by the mysterious Mr. Marshall whom Mrs. Keenan
described as being so "very kind" to her daughter.

Billy had been the one to discover the body. She had
reported for work at eleven o'clock that morning, her
customary time, noticed the coats on the floor and had

hurried to the bedroom. As soon as she saw her position on the bed, she realized that her mistress was dead. She touched her feet and they were cold. She also placed her hand inside the bosom and said the body there was still warm. The maid hurried out and notified a patrolman. She also telephoned Mrs. Keenan.

From the maid's observation of the warmth in the breasts, Dr. Norris was able to estimate that death probably occurred between seven and eight o'clock that morning.

Dot King's real name was Anna Marie Keenan. She was twenty-nine years old when murdered. She had been married to Eugene Oppel, a chauffeur, when she was eighteen, but they had separated a year or so later and she had finally obtained an Enoch Arden divorce. She was a beautiful girl, with blond wavy hair, blue eyes, and an exquisite figure. She became a model in a dress-making house at twenty-five dollars a week, soon began entertaining visiting buyers, and became a familiar figure along the gay spots of Broadway. She moved to the Great Northern Hotel, gave up her job, assumed the Dot King name, and became the mistress of various men. When she met Mr. Marshall, he installed her in the West Fifty-seventh Street apartment.

When Mrs. Keenan learned that her daughter had been murdered, she promptly furnished police with the name of a suspect. It was not the kind Mr. Marshall but Albert Guimares, whom it seems the kind Mr. Marshall was unwittingly supporting. Guimares, a swarthy man, who said he was Puerto Rican, was Dot King's real lover, and as is typical with many of these Broadway butterflies, she was supporting him, showering him with expensive

gifts and with much of the cash she was receiving from
Mr. Marshall. Mrs. Keenan said that he was brutal to
her daughter and frequently beat her.

The maid had an interesting tidbit to add. She said
that Dot King had had lunch with Mr. Marshall the previous afternoon and upon her return to the apartment had
telephoned Guimares and told him, "Daddy has been
more than generous. Do you know what he brought me,
Babe? A one-thousand-dollar Liberty bond, five hundred
dollars in cash, and the most marvelous jade and diamond
bracelet you ever saw, from Cartier's." The maid then
heard them quarreling, and Dot King began crying
as she refused to agree with whatever Guimares was
demanding.

There was a sheet of paper on the floor near the bed.
It was a will and read, "I, Dorothy Keenan, believing that
something unforeseen might happen to me, hereby be-
queath all my earthly possessions to my mother." A second duplicate will, this one bound in black paper and
the last page held down by a black silk ribbon sealed
with black wax, was on a small dressing table at the foot
of the bed. Still another exact copy of this will was
in a closed drawer of the same dressing table. None was
signed, and Mrs. Keenan said she knew nothing about
the documents. Dot had called to see her two days before
and told her nothing about making a will. The girl did
tell her mother that she was planning to buy her a bunga-
low in the country.

Mrs. Keenan said that Mr. Marshall had telephoned
the apartment at noon and she told him that Dot was
dead. He hung up immediately.

It was at this point that I left with Dr. Norris, and he

went to the morgue where he performed an autopsy. Death was due to chloroform, and there were bruise marks about the girl's mouth and slight abrasions inside the lower lip where the killer had held the saturated wad of cotton.

With the information of the elevator operator that Mr. Marshall still was in the apartment at seven o'clock in the morning when he went off duty, and the probable time of the murder set at between 7:00 and 8:00 A.M., the mysterious millionaire was the prime suspect, and police began the task of trying to identify him.

There were no signs of forced entry into the apartment and there were only two keys, the one carried by Dot King and the other by the maid. Billy said neither Guimares nor Mr. Marshall had a key to the apartment.

Guimares was picked up at his hotel and taken into custody. He said that the previous night he had been with friends until after two o'clock. He then had gone to bed, waking up after 9:00 A.M. It was not much as an alibi, but at the same time police could not disprove it. Because a gun was found in his room, he was held for violation of the Sullivan Law.

The search for the millionaire came to an end when he appeared voluntarily at the district attorney's office. He said that he had been at the Ritz-Carlton Hotel when he telephoned Dot to ask her to lunch. After learning from her mother that she was dead, he went to Wilson's office and conferred with him. They decided to hire a private detective to discover what had happened. It was this man who had called me at the medical examiner's office and aroused my suspicion.

When they learned from the late afternoon papers

that Dot King had been murdered, they consulted Neilson Olcott, a well-known lawyer, and on the following morning went with him to the district attorney's office where they were interviewed by Ferdinand Pecora. Inspector Coughlin, head of the detective bureau, was called in to take part in the conference.

Marshall said that he had been with Dot King until two o'clock in the morning. He stated she had been in good spirits when he left. He had gone down in the elevator. He freely admitted his relationship with the girl.

Pecora later issued a statement to reporters in which he said that the man known as Mr. Marshall, who was the last known person to have been with the murdered woman, had been to his office, and in the presence of Chief Inspector Coughlin had identified himself. Pecora's statement added that Mr. Marshall had been so frank and open with the authorities that they had eliminated him from any connection with the case.

The reporters, who also had interviewed Thomas, the elevator operator, and had received from him the same story he told me, pointed out that Marshall's statement that he had left by elevator at 2:00 A.M. did not agree with statements made by Thomas. Pecora said he had confronted Marshall with the elevator operator and that Marshall had reminded Thomas that he had given him a two-dollar tip when he took him down. The elevator operator had been somewhat uncertain about the incident.

The reporters asked for the identity of Mr. Marshall and were told by Pecora that he would not reveal the man's name, or that of Mr. Wilson, because he did not want to embarrass them and it would only hurt Mr. Marshall's family.

The newsmen were furious. Whether right or wrong, they felt they were witnessing one brand of justice for the rich and another for the poor. Guimares' lawyer helped add fuel to the feeling when he issued his own statement to the newspapermen in which he said, "They protect Marshall, who, according to his own admission, could easily have murdered Dot King, yet they hold my client in ten thousand dollars' bail on a phony charge and don't dare even insinuate that he killed Dot King."

The result was inevitable. Within twenty-four hours the public was less concerned about who had killed the butterfly girl than it was in getting the answer to the intriguing question, "Who is Mr. Marshall?"

Although I admit I had a normal curiosity and wondered myself about the identity of Mr. Marshall, this was not my reason for going to Dr. Norris and urging him to conduct his own inquiry into the case, as he had the authority to do under the law. The medical examiner's office is a separate agency that is not under the control of the police or the district attorney, and I felt that under the circumstances our office should hold a public inquiry into the murder of Dot King. Since Dr. Norris always had refused to hold any inquests, he told me it was up to the police and the district attorney to solve the case.

Information was given to reporters indicating that Dot King might have been killed because she was resisting someone who wanted to blackmail Mr. Marshall. This would account for the strangely worded unsigned will. The maid was quoted as having overheard some man tell

Dot King, "If you don't kick in, someday, by God, I'll toss you. We can make a real killing with this prize sap. All we need is a couple of them letters, and, by God, you'd better come across."

Just the day before she died Dot King was supposed to have told her masseuse, "I'll never stand for blackmailing my sugar daddy."

Police said that Mr. Marshall had written letters to Dot King but they had found only one in the apartment. It read: "Darling Dottie: Only two more days before I will be in your arms. I want to see you, oh, so much, and kiss your pretty pink toes."

Another man suddenly entered the case. He was Draper M. Daugherty, son of Harry M. Daugherty, the United States Attorney General in President Harding's cabinet. Daugherty told reporters that he had been one of the men in Dot King's life and that Francis Keenan, one of Dot's brothers, was trying to blackmail him.

"I was with Dot one night," he said, "and she introduced me to her brother. Half-kidding, I promised to get him a job with the United States Secret Service, and now he says that if I don't make good he'll expose my connection with his sister."

A short time later Daugherty's wife and his uncle, a brother of the Attorney General, had him committed to a sanitarium in Connecticut as a "dipsomanic and incorrigible alcohol addict." That swift action removed him from the case.

Reporters were told a trifle too much when it was mentioned that Mr. Marshall had telephoned Dot King from the Ritz-Carlton Hotel on the day her body had been found. One enterprising newsman, by methods he refused to reveal later to his crestfallen rivals, managed to obtain a list of all the telephone calls made from the switchboard in the hotel that day. Thumbing through the many slips, he found one that matched Dot King's telephone number. The slip gave the name of the man to whom the call had been charged. He immediately took a train to Philadelphia and appeared at the imposing home of J. Kearsley Mitchell, a Princeton alumnus, a clubman of Philadelphia, Boston, New York, Newport and Palm Beach. Mitchell, a man in his fifties, was married to Frances B. Stotesbury, the daughter of Edward B. Stotesbury, Philadelphia bank partner of J. P. Morgan. He was president of the Philadelphia Rubber Works Company and a director of many large corporations.

The reporter informed Mitchell that he had traced him through his telephone call to Dot King and bluntly told him he was going to publish his information. Mitchell then admitted that he was the mysterious Mr. Marshall. Mr. Wilson, his so-called secretary, was really John J. Jackson, a well-known New York lawyer who served both as his private and his business counsel.

When the story broke exclusively in this reporter's paper, Pecora then admitted to other reporters that Mitchell was the man he had been trying to save from embarrassment.

With Mitchell's name out in the open, witnesses again were questioned. Thomas now positively remembered that Mitchell had given him a two-dollar tip and that he had taken him down at two o'clock in the morning. I do not know how many users of that elevator had been in the habit of tipping the operator. I do know that it is not too ordinary a custom and I wonder why Thomas could not remember it the same day it was given.

Mrs. Keenan and Billy, the maid, now identified the comb found on the bed as belonging to Dot King. There were short hairs, typical of combings from a man's head, caught in the teeth.

Police began to lean to the theory that Dot King might have been killed by a burglar. I know that the captain in charge of the homicide squad did advance this theory in a book he wrote after he retired from the force. The maid said that a patent-leather suitcase was missing along with all of Dot's jewelry, valued at fifteen thousand dollars, the five hundred dollars in cash she had received the previous afternoon from Mitchell, fine dresses and lingerie, plus a light summer ermine coat and a fur cape. The two coats found on the foyer floor, according to this theory, were discarded because they would not fit into the crammed suitcase.

There was no ready explanation of how the thieves had gained admittance, since there were only two keys to the apartment, and no doors or windows showed any signs of being forced.

Police did not mention to reporters in discussing the possibility of a burglary the story told me by the maid that Mrs. Keenan had left the apartment with some of her daughter's things. The officer who did not notice the signs of murder evidently did not inspect or notice what was being taken out.

Mitchell did supply cynical reporters with one amusing moment. The knowledgeable head of a large corporation was shocked and surprised to learn that Dot King was seeing other men between his visits even though he was keeping her in an apartment. He had been lavish with her. In their year together he had given her more than ten thousand dollars in cash, paid all her bills, and given her all her jewelry, furs and frocks. At one point, hoping to improve her speech, he had hired an English tutor, but Dot King was no Liza Doolittle and after several lessons she chased the man out of her apartment.

Guimares profited considerably from Dot's association with Mitchell. She gave him a thirteen-hundred-dollar platinum watch, a seven-hundred-dollar fur overcoat, thirty-five dollar Oriental silk pajamas, and with the cash he received from her, he opened a brokerage office. When he was arrested, he was wearing diamond cuff links which Mitchell had given to Dot and which she had handed over to him.

Not long after, Pecora stated that if no arrest was made for the murder he would be forced to return to the routine of his office. No arrest was made, and the investigation petered out.

Dot's mother inherited what the girl left and disappeared soon after the services of a former assistant district attorney had been retained. None of the missing jewels, furs or clothing was ever found in any pawnshop.

The Mitchells closed their home and sailed for an extended visit abroad. Guimares was released, arrested for using the mails to defraud and was sent to the federal prison in Atlanta.

I do believe that under the old system of the coroner's court and inquest, the Dot King murder might have been solved. At least there would have been no withholding of the names of witnesses, and all those involved would have received a subpoena and been forced to tell

their stories under oath, making later changes more difficult to explain.

There are many unanswered questions in the case.
I would like the answer to three: Who drew up the three
unsigned wills and where were they drawn and typed?
What became of the missing jewelry and furs? Who
owned the pocket comb?

I suppose it is too late for any answers now and it
would make little difference to the once-gay girl who
rests under a modest marker in a cemetery.

CHAPTER FOURTEEN

Politics à la Carte

UNLIKE DR. CHARLES
Norris, who throughout his regime as chief medical examiner feared and distrusted politicians, I did not think
all of them were evil and corrupt men. In fact, my interest
in politics that began while I was a youth never slackened
during the thirty-six years I was with the office, and I
took an active part in all the campaigns through the
Latin-American political organization I had founded.
The ebb and flow of politics in this greatest city in the
world was a constant source of fascination for me.

I was not in politics for my personal benefit, for what
I could get out of it. On many occasions important political leaders told me to come to their office and offered
me well-paying jobs within the city administration, but
I was happy in my work and did not want to leave.

Even during my early years in office, when I still

thought of my job as a temporary one, I resisted tempting offers to work elsewhere for more money.

In 1899, when Henry Flagler was building a railroad through what was then the tropical jungle of Florida, he was faced with a serious shortage in help. He spoke to Thomas F. Crimmins, a prominent contractor, who suggested that Flagler get in touch with me. Flagler sent me a telegram at the coroner's office saying that he needed five hundred laborers at once and asked that I get in touch with him at his office at 26 Broadway. I knew nothing of his conversation with Crimmins, and Flagler's name meant nothing to me, so I pushed the telegram aside.

That night I happened to meet Crimmins, and he asked me if I had seen Flagler. He was surprised when I expressed my lack of knowledge of the man.

"Why, don't you know that he is John D. Rockefeller's partner in Standard Oil?" he asked. "He's building up the east coast of Florida and needs laborers. I thought you could round up some men for him."

Through my activities with minority groups I was well known among Italians, and since there were many immigrants arriving almost daily and they needed work, I realized this represented a good opportunity to help these people. The Italian banks on Mulberry and Elizabeth Streets served as a focal center. They exchanged American money for Italians returning to their native land, sent money abroad for men who had relatives in Italy, wrote letters for those who were illiterate, and even helped get them employment. I soon received pledges from these bankers of a sufficient number of men to meet the demand and went to see Flagler.

After all arrangements had been completed, Flagler

said to me, "Young man, I want you to cast your lot with us in Florida. We need a man who can deliver in our organization." Despite his urgings, I thanked him and left.

Not long after this, Isaac Guggenheim of the mining dynasty offered me double my salary to work for him, but I found the drama, the pathos, even the comedy of the coroner's office so absorbing and ever-changing that I would not leave.

Today, as I write this, I am nearing my one hundredth birthday. During the winter months I live in West Palm Beach, not far from the railroad and the mansion Flagler had built. In the summer I live on Long Island, where the Guggenheims live in many estates. I still wonder whether I was wise or foolish in turning down those legitimate offers.

I was able to use my political connections on two occasions, both times for the benefit of the medical examiner's office and Dr. Norris.

Toward the close of his first year in office, Dr. Norris had to appear before Mayor Hylan and the board of estimate to submit his budget for 1919. He asked for several additional stenographers and technicians and for a department automobile. Because we lacked funds, Dr. Norris was paying for the stenographer at the morgue out of his own pocket, and the office was using his private car for official calls to rush staff members to the scene of important cases.

One of the important members of Hylan's administration at that time was a former coroner who had lost his post when the office was abolished. The mayor knew little about the medical examiner's office and he turned

to this former coroner, who had been a plumber, for
advice and guidance. I might add that this ex-plumber
probably knew even less than the mayor did about the
office because he never had more than a hazy idea of
what the coroner's office was about when he served in it.
Dr. Norris, who always spoke out his mind, and had
a dislike for politicians anyway, listened to several remarks made by the former coroner and disrupted the
budget hearing by telling this man he was totally ignorant
and that he would not answer any more questions. Mayor
Hylan then demanded that Dr. Norris apologize to this
man and to the board.

The Chief looked at both of them, picked up his hat
and walked out of the room.

When the appropriations were announced, our office
was denied any of the funds requested. Without saying
a word to any of us, Dr. Norris wrote out his resignation
and sent it over to City Hall. I learned about it from an
agitated clerk in the mayor's office. I knew the loss of
Dr. Norris would be a tragic one to the city, since he
already was beginning to achieve excellent results. I
decided to act on my own. I went to see one of the city
commissioners, who was an important political leader,
and explained the situation to him. He asked just one
question: "Are those funds necessary?" I told him they
were needed for the proper functioning of the office. He
said he would go right in and speak to the mayor. When
he returned he told me that Hylan would like to talk
to Dr. Norris, and I set up an appointment for the following day. I then went to Dr. Norris and told him
about it.

Dr. Norris kept this appointment and was smiling

broadly when he returned. The mayor had refused to accept his resignation, told him he had heard he was doing good work and assured him that the additional help he wanted would be supplied.

The board did vote most of the funds at its next meeting. The money for the car had to be voted for by the board of aldermen. Our old friend, the ex-plumber, ex-coroner, was a member of this board. He spoke against the proposal and convinced his fellow aldermen to vote it down. Dr. Norris didn't care particularly; he was accustomed to paying for it himself anyway. But I knew it wasn't fair to our office; if anything happened to Dr. Norris, or to his car, we would be stranded when time could be very important in an investigation.

Once again I decided to intervene. This time I went to see C. F. Murphy, the head of Tammany Hall. He was surprised to learn that Dr. Norris was without an official car and asked who had blocked it. I told him. He said that Dr. Norris was too valuable a man for the city to lose. Several days later I received word from him to send our request for a car to the next meeting of the aldermen and it would be passed. I did and it was passed. Everybody, including the former coroner, voted for it; he had his orders.

Dr. Norris found it difficult to understand why a political leader had extended himself when it was no secret that no politician could hope for favors from him. I told him there were two kinds of political bosses, those interested in good government and those concerned only with lining their own pockets. I met examples of both kinds in my years in New York City politics.

It seems to me that politics today is a grim and joyless

business compared to those days in the 1880's when I cast my first vote. Perhaps it is just nostalgia for days that are gone forever, but the television screen is a poor substitute for the excitement of parades and bands and the speakers who appealed to our emotions as well as our intellects. We had fun out of our political battles. When we predicted the ruin of the nation if some rascal wasn't turned out, we did it with tongue in cheek. We knew our country was sturdy enough to survive even us.

I mentioned earlier how I had founded the Franco-American Democratic Club and later changed it to the Latin-American club to include Italian and Spanish voters. While we were largely members of the Democratic party, we had no hesitation in changing to Republican when we liked the candidate better. When Theodore Roosevelt ran for President, we backed him and became the Latin-American League. Some years after he had left the White House and had made his famous African hunting trip, I was appointed by Mayor Gaynor to a reception committee, all members of which were distinguished with the exception of me, to welcome him back to this country.

The reception committee members boarded the U. S. revenue cutter, *Androscoggin,* at 7:00 A.M. and went down the harbor to Quarantine where we were to meet the former President. Cornelius Vanderbilt, who was chairman of the committee, greeted Mr. Roosevelt as he stepped on board our cutter. Teddy seemed to know a great deal about every member of the committee. He strode along shaking hands with each member and added a personal remark. When he reached me he surprised me by asking, "LeBrun, how's the Latin-American League?" I told him we still were for him. When the cutter landed he was driven up Broadway in one of the first ticker-tape parades.

In 1896 when the Democrats nominated William Jennings Bryan, our organization was opposed to his silver policy and we backed McKinley. As an example of how politics operated then, there were two Italian newspapers in New York at that time, the largest being *Il Progresso*. It was the first Italian newspaper in this country and was owned by Carlo Barsotti. Barsotti had received an offer of three thousand dollars from the Democratic party if he would back their candidates. He told me he was willing to have his paper support the opposition but he wanted seven thousand dollars and asked me to submit his offer to the Republican National Committee. I did and the committee turned it down in favor of an Italian daily published in Chicago. Such a practice was not considered unusual at all at the time and caused no lifted eyebrows. It was at Barsotti's home where I attended a luncheon given for Caruso. It was the first time I met the great singer. The gathering was small, and he had many humorous stories to tell of feuds between noted opera stars.

For the McKinley campaign we had changed our name to the Latin-American Reform Union. Two years later, during the municipal campaign, the one in which Zucca was nominated for coroner, we were back under the Democratic banner and were known as the Latin-American Democratic League.

It was after my entrance into the coroner's office that I became acquainted with most of the Tammany district leaders. They usually came calling to seek some favor for one of their constituents in trouble.

Tom Foley, one of the best known of these leaders, owned a saloon opposite the old Criminal Courts Building that was a favorite meeting place for judges and lawyers as well as for city officials and politicians.

Early in 1902, during a gambler's quarrel, a man was shot in a café located in the Rossmore Hotel on the west side of Broadway at Forty-second Street. It was a place with an unsavory reputation frequented by sporting men and gamblers. The man who was shot was a notorious confidence man and cardsharp. His killer was a gambler.

The man was arrested and lodged in the Tombs to await the inquest. Coroner Scholer, a Republican, had charge of the case, and I was secretary to Scholer. Tom Foley came to see me and said the man who did the shooting had never been in trouble and that he wanted to help him. Although he did not request it, I knew he wanted to have the man admitted to bail. Since Scholer was of the opposition party, he did not want to go to him directly.

At the inquest several witnesses testified that they saw the victim make an attempt to pull something from his pocket before he was shot. The jury found that the shooting was in self-defense, and this verdict enabled the coroner, if he so desired, to admit the accused to bail to await the action of the grand jury. I then went to Scholer, told him of Foley's interest, and he agreed to admit the man to bail. Foley supplied the security.

Later District Attorney Jerome dismissed the indictment. Jerome, who was no friend of Tammany Hall, said of Foley, "His word is as good as his bond to me. He has never deceived me. He does much to get his people to go straight; this is my estimate of a man high in the councils of Tammany." There were never any political scandals attached to Foley and he was known for his many charitable acts. It did not matter to him whether a hungry or jobless man was a voter or how he registered. If he needed help, he got it.

And to Foley must go the credit for seeing the political possibilities of a young man named Alfred E. Smith and for starting him on his career.

I first met Al Smith in 1903, the same year he was nominated for the assembly, and at Foley's request worked for his election among the Italians in his district. During his first two years in Albany, Smith was disappointed. He felt submerged and that he never would be able to make his mark in that spot. His salary was only $125 a month and he had to pay his living expenses out of that, as well as maintain his family on Oliver Street.

He went to Foley and asked for a better paying job, but the political leader turned him down. "I gave you the nomination to represent the district so you could make a name for yourself. You can't do that in a couple of sessions."

Smith went back to Albany, and the talent Foley had recognized began to emerge. He was to become majority leader of the assembly, speaker, four times governor of the state, and finally his party's candidate for President.

In 1915, after serving all that time in the assembly on the meager salary, Smith pleaded for an opportunity to be able to support his family and he was given the nomination for sheriff, which was worth fifty thousand or more a year to the incumbent. He served for two years and was the last fee sheriff; the office was placed on a straight salary after that. Al Smith then became president of the board of aldermen on the same ticket with Hylan. He was not in sympathy with the policies of the mayor.

I was present when the boom to run him for governor began. He had asked me to come to see him. A clerk in our office was slated to be released, and Al Smith asked if I could keep him on for several weeks until he could find a new job for him. The budget funds were there and I agreed. When I first entered his office he was talking on the telephone and I heard him say, "Ah, now, cut out that governor stuff."

After he hung up I remarked that somebody evidently wanted him for the chief executive of the state.

"Yes," replied Al, "some of my old friends want me to get the nomination. I was just talking to an upstate leader, but I told him that there wasn't a chance, that I couldn't win even if I got the nomination."

Smith had underestimated his own popularity. He not only received the nomination but won the election. The leaders of Tammany Hall deliberately remained in the background during the campaign so that they could not be an issue. For this election I also organized the Allied Democratic League. One of the active workers for Smith was Mrs. Belle Moskowitz, and he was so impressed with her ability that after his election he induced her to come to Albany, where she served as his valuable assistant for many years. It was Mrs. Moskowitz who introduced Smith to Robert Moses, whom he appointed State Park Commissioner. Smith's strong support of Moses led to the eventual development of the world-famous Jones Beach and Long Island's beautiful parkway system.

When Al Smith was nominated for the Presidency in

1928, our organization, which finally settled into its permanent name of the Latin-American Democratic League, supported him. I heard that Henry Morgenthau was going to stump for Governor Smith and attack the Kellog-Briand multilateral treaties. I wrote to John R. Rascob, chairman of the National Democratic Committee, and protested that such an attack would be detrimental to Smith, particularly among the foreign groups, who believed the treaties were at least an effort for world peace. I was told that the matter would be considered and Mr. Morgenthau did not attack the treaties in any speeches during the campaign. I think our country was the loser when Smith was not elected; he would have made a great President.

A different kind of political leader was George Washington Plunkett, who controlled a district centered at Eighth Avenue and Fiftieth Street. When I met him he had become a wealthy man, had been a contractor and had served in the state senate. He was pleasant-speaking, wore a beard and mustache and always carried a cane. He did not drink liquor, but he was a cigar smoker. Five days a week he could be found sitting on one of the bootblack stands in the courthouse, and he liked to talk about his political philosophy. This is an actual interview he gave.

I set out, when I cast my first vote, to win fame and money in New York politics. Did I offer my services to the district leader as a stump speaker? Not much. The woods are full of such speakers. Did I get up a book on municipal government and show it to the leader? I wasn't such a fool. What I did was to get some marketable goods before going to the leader. I had a cousin, a young man, who didn't take any particular interest in politics. I went to him and said, "Tommy, I'm going to be a politician, and I want to get a following. Can I count on you?" He said, "Sure, George." That's how I started in business. I got a marketable commodity—one vote. Then I went to the district leader and told him I could command two votes on election day, Tommy's and my own. He smiled on me and told me to go ahead. If I had offered him a speech or a book full of learning, he would have said, 'Oh, forget it.' That was the beginning in a small way, wasn't it? But that is the only way to become a real lasting statesman.

I soon branched out. Two young men in the flat next to mine were school friends. I went to them, just as I went to Tommy, and they agreed to stand by me. Then I had a following of three votes and I began to get a bit chesty. Whenever I dropped into district headquarters, everybody shook hands with me, and the leader one day honored me by lighting a match for my cigar. And so it went like a snowball rolling downhill. I worked the flat house that I lived in from the basement to the top floor, and I got about a dozen men to follow me. Before long I had sixty men back of me and formed the George Washington Plunkett Association.

What did the district leader say when I called at headquarters? He came after me and said, "George, what do you want? If you don't see what you want, ask for it. Wouldn't you like to have a job in the departments for your friends?" I said, "I'll think it over. I haven't decided yet what the George Washington Plunkett Association will do in the next campaign." You ought to have seen how I was courted and petted then by the leaders of the rival organizations. I had marketable goods and there were bids for them from all sides, and I was a rising man in politics. As time went on, and my association grew, I thought I would like to go to the assembly. I just had to hint at what I wanted. Afterwards, I went to the board of aldermen, then to state senate, then became leader of the district, and so on up, till I became statesman.

This self-styled statesman had one pet hate—civil service.

It would be all a mess if every man who wanted a job would have to run up against a civil service examination. I know more than one young man in past years who worked for the ticket and was just overflowing with patriotism, but when he was knocked by the civil service humbug he got to hate this country and became an anarchist.

My first meeting with William Randolph Hearst took place in 1905 when he ran for mayor of New York on an independent ticket against George B. McClellan. I met Max Ihmsen, one of Hearst's star reporters, in the lobby of the Hoffman House, and he urged me to have the Latin-American Democratic League support the publisher. I told him we had committed our support to McClellan. Even so, he urged me to come upstairs where Hearst had his campaign headquarters to meet him. The publisher was pleasant during our brief chat. McClellan won by a small plurality. Hearst insisted there had been frauds and asked for a recount. It was granted, and McClellan was declared elected by a scant 3,476 votes. The publisher probably was right in saying that the election had been stolen from him.

McClellan blamed Tammany for his narrow victory, claiming the organization had not worked for him, and broke with Murphy, the Tammany boss. This was a mistake. The leaders had done their best, but the East Side was solidly for the publisher, and his picture was displayed in the windows of almost every tenement. If McClellan had not broken with Murphy, he probably would have been the next gubernatorial candidate, a post that has led to the White House.

In the vagaries of politics, Murphy turned about-face and obtained the nomination of Hearst for governor, and

I met the publisher for a second time. Our League supported him in this race, but he was defeated by Charles
E. Hughes.

Despite the various political campaigns, whether I was
for Hearst or against him, his papers always supported
my campaigns to help save lives and in that way certainly
fulfilled an important public function.

I helped give Grover Whalen his start in politics. I had
known his father, Michael, during the first years I was in
the coroner's office. He had two sons, Stevenson and
Grover. I believe Grover was named after Grover Cleveland, the father having held a position in the United
States Custom House under Cleveland's administration.

It was during the mayoralty campaign of 1913, with
Judge McCall running against John P. Mitchell, that
Stevenson and Grover invited me to lunch. I was at the
McCall headquarters in charge of the bureau of voters
of foreign birth and descent. The brothers told me they
would like to take part in the campaign, and I gave their
names to the committee at headquarters. Grover Whalen
evidently liked his taste of politics, even though McCall
lost, and I next met him when he was active in Hylan's
campaign for mayor. Grover acted as Hylan's secretary
and accompanied him to all meetings he had to attend.

There was little outstanding about the Hylan administration. It was conducted more honestly than had been
expected. He had two obsessions. One was the retention
of the five-cent subway fare, and the other was his constant bombardment of department heads on the necessity for economy. I had written to him asking for a salary
increase for an elderly clerk in his sixties who both needed
and deserved a raise. In reply I got this letter from
Mayor Hylan:

"This clerk, instead of trying to get his salary increased, he should first have the interest of the city in his mind. If he does, who knows, but some day, he may become great and become Mayor of the City?"

Grover Whalen served for a time as official secretary to Mayor Hylan. World War I had ended in the first year of his administration, soldiers were returning, and many distinguished visitors were arriving in the city. The mayor named a group of prominent citizens, including city officials, to serve as a reception committee.

Grover had inherited his father's contracting business which carted ashes and debris away from many Broadway buildings. One of these was the John Wanamaker store, and Grover suggested to Hylan that Rodman Wanamaker be named chairman of the committee. After that Grover accompanied Rodman Wanamaker whenever any distinguished guest arrived, and in time he took on the post and became the most celebrated greeter of celebrities.

While I was president of the League, a young man named Carmine DeSapio joined the organization. He was the protégé of Michael A. Scudi, who was secretary of our club.

One day Scudi brought DeSapio to my office and said the young man was seeking the position of secretary to one of the city court judges and they asked my help in obtaining the endorsement of John F. Curry, the Tammany Hall leader. I pointed out that all such positions had to have the endorsement of the leader of the district in which the applicant lived, that Curry would not go over a district leader's head. In this case it was Dan Finn, and DeSapio did not have his endorsement.

Not long after this visit, DeSapio did obtain the appointment. Scudi told me that DeSapio himself had maneuvered to get one of the judges to appoint him as secretary. He later ran for leader of his district against Dan Finn and defeated him. The district had many Italian-Americans living in it.

When Mayor O'Dwyer ran for his second term, the late Generoso Pope was treasurer of his campaign committee and many other Italians were actively supporting the campaign. The real leadership of Tammany Hall at that time was vacant and was being filled on a temporary basis by Hugo Rogers, who was borough president of Manhattan. Pope and the others prevailed on O'Dwyer to name one of the Italian district leaders as the head of the Democratic organization.

Two of these men were discussed for leadership. They were former Judge Francis X. Mancuso and Carmine DeSapio. Mancuso was eliminated, and DeSapio, leader of the first district, was elected.

Some sixty years after I had founded the Latin-American organization and had demanded a place on the ticket for the first Italian to be elected to a city office in New York, a former member of the organization had become the leader of Tammany Hall. The wheel of politics had taken its full turn.

In the never-ending kaleidoscope that is politics in New York, DeSapio is now out of office and a new cycle will begin. With the granddaughter of a former member in the White House, perhaps a man of French descent will yet become the Democratic leader in New York.

When I retired from the medical examiner's office, I began to divide my time between Florida and Long Island I no longer lived in New York City and ceased my active association with politics.

My years of experience brought home several lessons to me. Despite the evil connotation the words "political boss," have in most people's minds, a political boss is necessary in our modern society to keep the actual wheels of government moving. A political boss does not have to be evil. There have been many public-minded men who served as political bosses and they were interested in good, clean and honest government. It takes only a few like Boss Tweed to bring an organization into such disrepute that it never really recovers and is always subject to attack and suspicion.

A corrupt political boss or a corrupt political machine, particularly at the local level, is due solely to the apathy and the indifference of the public, the voters themselves. Political bosses like the power the position gives them. They don't want to lose that power and they will give the voters what they want to stay in power. If the voters demand good government, they will get it.

It also has become fashionable over the years for most young men to avoid becoming involved in politics. If you hand over by default the fundamental operations of politics to those who are only seeking something for themselves, you cannot expect political machines to be concerned about the public. Politics needs a constant infusion of new blood, new ideas and enthusiasm. It has produced some of the great leaders of our country. It should continue to do so.

CHAPTER FIFTEEN

Personal

WHEN A MAN REACHES the age of one hundred years, interest is expressed in his longevity. I can only be a disappointment to the faddists and theorists.

To teetotalers, I must remind them that I am of French descent and that I learned at an early age the delights of a good glass of wine. It is only within the last few years that I no longer have a daily drink but reserve it for important occasions. My grandchildren think there are too many important occasions.

I have no sympathy with Prohibition. Many may recall those days as the era of gangsters or of flappers. I was in the medical examiner's office then and I still recall with horror the thousands of lives lost because of poisoned alcohol masquerading as just-off-the-boat liquor.

For those who decry the evils of nicotine, I offer my regrets that my life cannot serve as an example. My first job at the age of eighteen was selling cigars. I smoked them then. I still do now.

Scientists have advanced the theory that longevity is due to heredity, and many people feel themselves doomed to an early death because one or both of their parents died young. For these people I can offer good cheer, not for the scientists. My mother died while still in her twenties, and my father was in his early forties when he died, as had his father before him. My oldest daughter was in her seventies when she developed high-blood pressure and was told by her doctor to cut down on her activities. She loved dancing and did not consider life worth while without it. She died as she may have wanted to go, while dancing.

If there is any secret to longevity, perhaps it is in having an interest in others. Even today I still take an interest in the organizations I helped found to save human lives. People are interesting and fascinating. By being interested in them, I do not have time to brood about myself, so I rarely become ill. When I do, I feel I am missing too many things and so am impatient to get well.

I take daily walks, enjoy automobile rides, and read the newspapers every day. I type my own letters. I noticed because of the heavy correspondence involved in writing this book that typing was not as easy as it once was. I shouldn't complain. I have had that typewriter for many years and I suppose it is getting old.

Index